Rob Long's

)OX

A Lucky Duck Book

Rob Long's
Intervention Toolbox

For Social, Emotional and Behavioural Difficulties

Los Angeles • London • New Delhi • Singapore • Washington DC

First published 2009

SAGE Publications Ltd
1 Oliver's Yard
55 City Road
London EC1Y 1SP

SAGE Publications Inc.
2455 Teller Road
Thousand Oaks, California 91320

SAGE Publications India Pvt Ltd
B 1/I 1 Mohan Cooperative Industrial Area
Mathura Road, Post Bag 7
New Delhi 110 044

SAGE Publications Asia-Pacific Pte Ltd
33 Pekin Street #02-01
Far East Square
Singapore 048763

www.luckyduck.co.uk

Library of Congress Control Number 2008934287

British Library Cataloguing in Publication data

A catalogue record for this book is available from the British Library

ISBN 978-1-4129-4605-6

Typeset by C&M Digitals (P) Ltd., Chennai, India
Printed in India by Replika Press, Pvt. Ltd
Printed on paper from sustainable resources

My thanks to all those who have helped me in the writing of this book. In particular Katie Metzler at Sage for her suggestions and contributions, and a special thanks to George Robinson for his invaluable review of the work in progress, which was both needed and appreciated.

To my family, Jenni, Joe and Olga, for being a constant source of love, fun and meaning. To Christine, my lasting gratitude for helping me choose wisely.

And finally, to all who carry the 'pebble', thanks, attitude is everything.

Contents

How to Use the CD-Rom

The CD-Rom contains PDF files of resources from the book separated by chapter. You will need Acrobat Reader version 3 or higher to view and print these pages.

The document is set to print at A4 but you can enlarge them to A3 by increasing the output percentage using the page set-up settings for your printer.

Throughout the book, you will see this CD icon used ⊙. This indicates that there is electronic material available on the CD-Rom.

All material on this CD-Rom can be printed off and photocopied by the purchaser/user of the book. The CD-Rom itself may not be reproduced or copied in its entirety for use by others without permission from SAGE Publications. Should anyone wish to use the materials from the CD-Rom for conference purposes, they would require separate permission from us. All material is © SAGE, 2009. The CD-Rom will enable staff to quickly have an overview of how to use the Toolbox, with specific worked-through examples.

Contents of CD-Rom

PowerPoint slides

Notes for the PowerPoint Presentation

A Road Map for Using the Toolbox

Chapter 4

The Dimension Questions

Tool Intervention Log

Chapter 5

Physiological

Tension Scale

Progressive Muscle Relaxation Script

Visualisation Exercise

Feelings

Record of My Successes!

The Quick Relax Method

Introduction

The difficulties that a significant number of children and young people display in schools is well documented. Palmer (2006) reports that over the past 30 years behavioural problems in young people have doubled and emotional problems have increased by some 70 per cent. The increases are seen to reflect the many changes that have taken place in our society. Changes in society are identified as significant in the increase in stressors on young people and an increase in the likelihood of disorders. Rutter and Smith (1995) found such factors as secularisation of society, the changing pattern of the family and the increased role of the mass media as each contributing towards an understanding of why we are witnessing more psychosocial disorders in young people.

To be an 'inclusive' school is to be a school that is seriously challenged to support children with a wide array of difficulties and conditions. Schools have a significant role to play, but it is naive to think that schools alone can solve these problems. Children grow up in a range of different social contexts and each context influences a child's development. Efforts must be made at all levels to effect lasting changes – families need to be supported, communities need to be actively involved and both need to liaise with schools. The problem behaviours that children develop say as much about the contexts in which these problem behaviours occur as they do about the child.

All behaviour is multidimensional, no one factor can explain everything. Problem behaviours especially, have a multitude of causes, and multifaceted problems need multifaceted solutions. Professionals that work at different levels – family, community, whole-school and classroom – can each increase the protective factors in children's lives and reduce the at risk ones. Too often one professional claims superiority over another, but it is not a question of which is best – each has a definite role to play. The Toolbox is written for those school practitioners who find themselves supporting children and young people who have problem behaviours that act as barriers to their successful engagement with school. Such staff can be faced with a wide array of concerns – anxiety, low self-esteem and disruptive behaviours as well as specific medical conditions such as attention deficit disorder, Tourette's syndrome, etc. Practical ideas will be given about such specific conditions but, more importantly, the Toolbox will provide an action research model with proven techniques to enable staff to design comprehensive support programmes.

So what does the Toolbox look like and how does it work?

Essentially it has six tool compartments or dimensions:

1 Physiological
2 Feelings
3 Behaviour
4 Cognitive
5 Social
6 Happiness.

For each compartment there are a number of tools – or interventions – that may be used, depending on age and level of understanding of the young person.

A Road Map for Using the Toolbox

Step 1

The problem is the problem, not the child.

Step 2

Using the assessment questionnaire in Chapter 4, a profile is produced.

Step 3

Dimensions scoring over 8 need interventions.

Step 4

A range of relevant tools, which are outlined in Chapter 5, are chosen and used to address the problem.

Step 5

A review is made using the assessment questionnaire to compare before and after outcomes. All problem behaviours have many component parts, not just one. This is partly

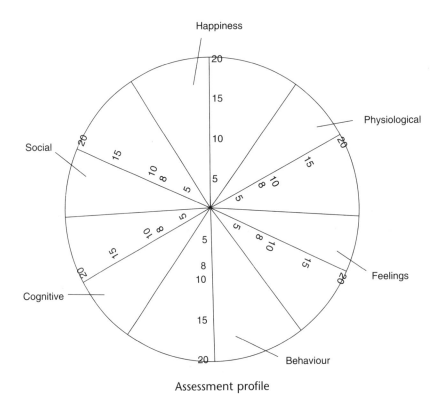

Assessment profile

why many interventions fail to be as effective as they could be because they take a standpoint that one tool fits all problems. The Toolbox enables us to employ several different tools that comprehensibly tackle the problem behaviour. So from the Toolbox the practitioner can take the most relevant interventions and place them in a 'string bag'. A string bag is ideal as it can become whatever shape it needs to be in order to fit the shape of the problem.

The degree of relevance that any particular tool has to a problem is decided by answering a set of indicative assessment questions. Usually all tools are used at some time, but some are used more frequently. Ideally, the young person is actively involved in the whole process, because it is the problem that is to be analysed, not the child. A useful way of remembering this is: the problem is the problem, not the child. Drawing on personal experience here are two examples.

Case Study 1

JJ is nine years old and her teachers complain about her slowness in completing assignments. She seems to need a lot of reassurance and will often cry in class during new assignments or group work. During playtimes JJ is seen wandering around alone, and would rather stay in and read than join in with other children. She often complains of feeling anxious and frightened.

For a moment consider how a car mechanic would begin to investigate a problem in a car engine and then transfer this approach to addressing JJ's problems. Through basic observation it can be seen immediately that there are clear indications that JJ will need a range of interventions, namely:

- Physiological tools – teaching her relaxation skills to help her cope with her physiological arousal.

- Feelings tools – skills to raise her feelings of self-worth and an understanding of her negative feelings.

- Behavioural tools – to explore the triggers that seem to lead to her crying in class, whether these can be changed or if JJ can be taught alternative coping responses.

- Cognitive tools – JJ will probably have negative thoughts, such as 'I'm not popular with other children' or 'Nobody wants to play with me', that will require techniques designed to develop positive thinking to eradicate.

- Social tools – JJ seems to lack friendship-making skills, so this would be an area to explore and perhaps help strengthen.

- Happiness tools – it is clear that she is not enjoying school. Interventions that can help her focus on the good things in school, as well as developing a 'badge of courage' as she faces her challenges will be of value.

The beginnings of a comprehensive intervention programme for JJ begin to emerge. Our Toolbox has provided us with a multifaceted approach that is much more likely to be effective in tackling the problem.

Returning to the car mechanic, we would expect that after listening to the car he would carry out some form of diagnostic testing, to provide more precise information. For us, the more detailed assessment will come through applying a set of indicative questions to the problem, which will be detailed later.

 ## Case Study 2

TS is 14 years old and has a history of social, emotional and behavioural difficulties. He has some in-class support, but his behaviour with certain teachers has deteriorated – refusing to comply with reasonable requests and often shouting out and banging his desk. His peer relationships have worsened and he has been reported for bullying some members of his tutor group. He is frequently sent out of lessons and his parents have been interviewed in school several times. Detentions and similar punishments seem to have little or no effect.

Once again it can be seen from the description of TS's problems that certain interventions will be needed to support him. This is the initial assessment, before

(Continued)

(Continued)

the set of indicative questions are completed. These questions will often confirm your first hunch, giving you added confidence in how to approach the problem.

It is important to remember that it is the answers given to the assessment questions that determine the interventions to be used. However, it would be foolish not to draw on the professional insight and understanding that every practitioner acquires through hands-on experience.

- Feelings – TS is receiving little positive feedback for his work and his relationship with adults and peers seems poor. This range of negativity is likely to have damaged his personal confidence, so some self-esteem activities would probably prove useful.

- Behaviour – there is a need to analyse the circumstances which lead to TS being excluded from classes. Is there a pattern to it? Are there certain triggers, and what are the consequences that follow? Does being excluded enable him to avoid work he does not like? Are there any positive consequences that could be employed to increase appropriate behaviour?

- Cognitive – does TS have doubts about his abilities in certain subject areas? Is there a need for some cognitive restructuring? That is, helping him to challenge negative thoughts about his ability and work. Also, as he sometimes hurts others a Restorative Justice approach could be used. That is, 'What have you done? What was the outcome? How can you make amends and learn what to do next time?'

- Socially – the fact that he is bullying other children will naturally damage his chance of having friends. In fact, children will naturally avoid him because of his bullying tendencies. Some social skills training might be of value to help TS understand how to make friends and relate better to others.

- Happiness – an area from which he could benefit – finding his signature strengths and enabling him to employ them would be positive, as well as other activities such as helping others and positive event planning.

As these two examples show, the Toolbox approach means that the many different aspects to a problem are dealt with in a constructive manner. This approach does not reject others, it merely utilises those aspects that appear most relevant for any problem behaviour. The approach is driven by the needs of the problem, not the needs of the theory upon which a technique is based. For example, if a purely behavioural approach was taken, there would be no need to be concerned with feelings. Similarly, a cognitive approach would not analyse behavioural patterns, but because specific individual problems are being analysed it can be seen that each problem has several elements to it.

Further Reading 📖

Clough, P., Garner, P., Pardeck, J.T. and Yuen, F. (eds) (2005) *Handbook of Emotional and Behavioural Difficulties*. London: SAGE.

Palmer, S. (2006) *Toxic Childhood*. London: Orion Books.

Porter, L. (2007) *Behaviour in Schools: Theory and Practice for Teachers*. Maidenhead: Open University Press.

1

Children and Young People in School

A growing amount of evidence highlights the rise in the incidence of childhood disorders:

> it is estimated that at least 10% of the school population in England is, at any one time, affected with social, emotional and behavioural difficulties ..., it is important to note that the overwhelming majority are to be found in mainstream schools. (Cooper, 2005)

There is an increase in 'acting out' disorders (behaviour/conduct disorders), as well as the 'acting in' emotional, mental health disorders (eating disorders, anxiety, depression, self-injury). Haggerty et al. (1996) spoke of 'many troubled families who share a multitude of risk factors', including genetic, biological and psychosocial factors, and that children suffer from these cumulative effects.

Whatever the explanation for these increases, there is hardly a teacher or support staff who does not recognise that they are faced with supporting an ever-increasing number of children with social, emotional and behavioural difficulties (SEBD). Schools make a significant difference for children with SEBD, and this book will give examples of how this can be achieved.

The first phase is essentially to have in place those factors that create the right school ethos. The second phase follows this through by setting up a school-wide behaviour team. The third phase is having in place an effective classroom behaviour plan. The fourth phase of the system is how to help learners who, despite the ethos, the school team and effective classroom management, have SEBD issues, and this phase will be the focus of the Toolbox.

The first three phases help the majority of learners engage successfully with the curriculum offered. Below is a brief account of what each of these phases might look like in an effective school.

Phase One – School Ethos

Some of the school factors that help create the right ethos are (Marzano, 2003b):

- Professionalism – there is strong and purposeful leadership with shared values that supports cooperation between staff.

- Curriculum – ensuring that all learners have the opportunity to learn through a viable curriculum.

- Goals and feedback – having challenging academic goals for all learners with agreed teaching methods and good monitoring helps build a whole-school approach.

- Home and community links – essentially there are three ingredients for the positive involvement of home and community:

  - good communication systems

  - opportunities for positive participation in activities

  - a degree of influence in decision making.

A Model Example

To establish the correct ethos, which is a fundamental aim of Phase One, the following steps could be undertaken by any school. If a secondary school has serious concerns regarding student behaviour, then the following steps could be a systematic plan to be undertaken over a three-year period.

The initial phase would test the current situation – 'What are the attitudes of staff towards behaviour?' A questionnaire would be used to determine staff views on such key aspects as:

- Do the staff believe that problem behaviour is caused by individuals, who have to be caught and punished? Or do they believe that staff should be proactive and plan strategies to prevent problem behaviour?

- Are the staff individualistic, believing that each member of staff has to depend on their own resources, or are they collaborative – believing in whole-school approaches?

A specific aim with regard to behaviour, would be to promote a belief in the staff that making mistakes and having to deal with the consequences is a common feature of managing behaviour. There are no simplistic solutions. Based on this initial data obtained, a whole-school development day would be planned to explore and establish core values.

Phase Two – School-wide Behaviour Team

The second phase is for the school to set up a school-wide behaviour team that manages behavioural issues. The most successful schools see inclusion as a real challenge and the inclusion of children with SEBD as the greatest challenge – but they appreciate the need for proactive techniques to enhance positive behaviour in all children. The stronger the positive influence – that is, staff energy mainly focused on increasing desirable behaviours, rather than trying to extinguish unwanted behaviours – the easier it is for all, and the few staff who need extra support are more readily identified.

The following headings could be guidelines towards creating an inclusive and proactive approach:

Step 1 Assemble a positive school-wide behaviour team

Over time, such a team would develop the expertise to support colleagues in analysing behaviour difficulties and implementing interventions.

Step 2 Assess school needs

Behavioural audits could be undertaken to indicate any 'hot spots' – curriculum areas or actual locations (corridors, etc.) – for poor behaviour that exist, as well as identifying those staff who make the most discipline referrals.

Step 3 Set goals

Based on hard data whole-school behavioural goals could be clearly defined.

Step 4 Select/design interventions

Using the team as a resource, a specific plan of action could now be proposed.

Step 5 Establish support

A clearly stated support network could be set up to cover whole-school, whole-class, staff and individual student issues. Those who are most directly affected by any specific problem behaviour could be included in the proposed action.

Step 6 Engage and train staff

The more staff that generally agree with the analysis of behaviour and the resulting way forward should make proposals easier to implement. Sharing the same core beliefs about behavioural matters is an important step.

Step 7 Implement, monitor and maintain

This will involve the established team and other key staff in setting up an agreed framework for introducing, monitoring and maintaining behavioural standards.

Step 8 Assess effectiveness

Alongside the monitoring of the plan, the effectiveness must also be evaluated and reviewed on a regular basis.

Phase Three – Classroom Behaviour Plan

It is the classroom teacher who controls the pacing, sequencing and general experiences that influence learners. Effective teachers create their desired learning environment through designing a variety of ways to deliver the curriculum. It follows that the more methods a teacher has to employ, the more effective their teaching will become.

For children to be included in any classroom there needs to be a definite plan of action on the part of the class teacher and support staff. This approach could ensure that protective factors are maximised for those learners who face SEBD; Kaiser and Rasminsky (2003) identified such factors as being:

- respect for self and others

- social interaction skills

- problem-solving skills.

To successfully include children who face SEBD, schools need to look at ways of creating an environment that enables them to be successful, despite their difficulties. It is not a question of 'fixing' them, it is a matter of asking how a school can promote their successful inclusion. However, what works well for learners with SEBD usually works well with all learners. Bloomquist and Schnell (2005) suggest the following key stages in a classroom behaviour plan.

Step 1 – Develop class guidelines.

Step 2 – Teach appropriate behaviours, for example, social and conflict resolution skills.

Step 3 – Effective use of rewards and consequences.

 Case Study 1.1

A class teacher having established her classroom procedures and routines, turned her attention to the effective use of rewards. She asked learners to complete a survey rating their preference for different rewards. These included:

- extra playtime
- a good note home
- classroom games
- free time
- watching a video
- listening to tapes
- computer time
- group games in gym.

Based on her findings she was able to develop a much more effective rewards system.

Schools that adopt this phased approach can systematically increase the likelihood of positive behaviour in learners. This should then reduce the number of problem behaviours that any school experiences.

The next phase is then the Toolbox, which enables practitioners to design intervention programmes for the many different types of SEBD that school staff will inevitably meet. However, in every school there will be a small but significant group that will need specialist support. This group of children display SEBD, but the main cause for their difficulties is usually medical in nature. The next chapter will look at some of the most frequent behavioural disorders that school staff are likely to meet with some suggestions as to how they can be supported in the classroom. The focus will then lead exclusively on to Phase Four, the multifaceted Toolbox.

Further Reading

Marzano, R. (2003a) *Classroom Management that Works: Research Based Strategies for Every Teacher.* Alexandria, USA: Association for Supervision and Curriculum Development.

Marzano, R. (2003b) *What Works in Schools: Translating Research into Action.* Alexandria, USA: Association for Supervision and Curriculum Development.

2

Common Childhood Behavioural Disorders

Definitions and Disorders

Being clear about what is meant when a pupil is said to have SEBD is a challenge in itself. What may be seen as a behaviour problem in one school is not necessarily in another. Behaviour that one class teacher will not accept can be happily tolerated by a colleague in the room next door.

A dictionary definition of disorder is to 'disarrange, throw into confusion; put out of health, upset' (*The Concise Oxford Dictionary*, 1956). Medically it indicates a group of symptoms, signs and pathological findings that are deviant from some standard of normality. With regard to children's behaviour, disorders are behaviours that adults in legally recognised authority do not like children to have and that occur more frequently than would be typical for a child of comparable age.

General Behavioural Disorders

Oppositional defiant disorder (ODD) – a pattern of negativistic, hostile and defiant behaviour lasting at least six months and including such behaviours as arguing with adults, defying adult requests, being spiteful and revengeful, and deliberately annoying to others. The average age for onset is six years.

Conduct disorder (CD) – a repetitive and persistent pattern of behaviour that violates the rights of others as well as the major age-appropriate social norms. Behaviours include aggression towards people and animals, destruction of property, deceitfulness or theft. Average age for onset is nine years.

If a child meets the criteria for both conditions they are diagnosed as having a conduct disorder. Most youngsters diagnosed with conduct disorder also meet the criteria for oppositional defiant disorder, but not all children with ODD go on to develop CD. An important point to make is that children and young people with ODD can be supported by the interventions that are offered by the Toolbox. But if a learner is diagnosed as having a conduct disorder then those professionals who have made such a diagnosis will advise school staff how best to support the individual.

It is worth noting that 35 to 70 per cent of children diagnosed as having attention deficit hyperactivity disorder (ADHD) will also develop ODD and between 30 and 50 per cent will develop CD. When this happens, ADHD usually precedes the other disorders.

What Causes Behaviour Disorders?

Current understanding of SEBD has greatly increased. We are much more aware of the 'at risk' factors that are associated with children developing behavioural problems. These include some of the following:

- Family factors: Nowadays there seems to be an ever-increasing list of 'at risk' family factors. The major factors will include family breakdown, abuse, bereavement, alcohol/drug abuse as well as mental illness, poor parenting and neglect.

- Community factors: For many children the neighbourhoods in which they live have few resources and can be dominated by delinquent peer groups, which in turn seem to be developing a gang culture, with their own values and beliefs.

While these factors are commonly associated with SEBD, a child can have SEBD with none of these present.

Common Medical Disorders

These are conditions that are considered to have mainly organic/biological causes. They are distinctive syndromes with specific symptoms, for example, attention deficit hyperactivity disorder (ADHD), autistic spectrum disorder, Asperger's and Tourette's syndrome. Because of the nature of these conditions children and young people may be on medication to treat some of the more prominent and disabling symptoms. School staff should liaise and work collaboratively in developing support programmes that will enable learners with specific conditions to maximise their opportunities in whichever educational setting they are placed.

Children with these conditions will not respond as other children do because of their additional difficuties. It is wrong and foolish to define inclusion for such children with an attitude of 'You can be with us only if you can be like us'. These children are unable to fit this criterion and this is not inclusion as it should be defined. Just as there is a differentiated learning curriculum, under such circumstances there is a need for a differentiated behavioural curriculum.

The two most common medical disorders that mainstream school staff can expect to meet are Asperger's syndrome and attention deficit hyperactivity disorder. After defining these conditions, an in-class behaviour plan will be suggested to assist school staff to include learners who are diagnosed and display these symptoms.

Asperger's Syndrome

Asperger's syndrome (AS) – also known as Asperger's disorder or autistic psychopathy – is a pervasive developmental disorder (PDD) characterised by severe and sustained impairment in social interaction, development of restricted and repetitive patterns of behaviour, interests and activities. These characteristics result in clinically significant impairment in social, occupational, or other important areas of functioning. In contrast to autistic disorder (autism), there are no clinically significant delays in language or cognition or self-help skills or in adaptive behaviour, other than social interaction. Prevalence is limited but it appears to be more common in males. Onset is later than is seen in autism, or at least recognised later. A large number of children are diagnosed between the ages of five and nine. Motor delays, clumsiness, social interaction problems, and idiosyncratic behaviours are reported. Adults with Asperger's have trouble with empathy and social interaction as these difficulties follow a continuous course into adulthood and are usually lifelong.

Asperger's is not easily recognisable, in fact, many children are misdiagnosed with other neurological disorders such as Tourette's syndrome or autism. More frequently, children are misdiagnosed with attention deficit (and hyperactivity) disorders, oppositional defiant disorder, or obsessive – compulsive disorder. Such mistakes in diagnosis can lead to a delay in treatment of the disorder. Many pharmaceuticals and natural remedies are used to treat multiple neurological and pervasive developmental disorders ranging from St John's Wort tea to drugs such as Haldol and Ritalin. Treatments vary to a great degree with the individual patient, no single medication or remedy works for everyone, and AS cannot be completely cured.

Some Common Features   Children with AS often find social interaction difficult as they fail to read social cues. This can result in individuals who have little motivation to develop peer relationships, which through lack of practice, only leads to an increase in social skills difficulties. There is also a tendency for them to become over absorbed in a narrow interest to the exclusion of other activities. It is not uncommon for routines to be followed obsessively.

Speech and language also develop in a specific manner. While speech can appear perfect, it is often over-formal and somewhat pedantic. The child with AS can struggle with understanding everyday colloquiums, for example, 'Pull your socks up' may be taken literally.

In-class Behaviour Plan for Learners with Asperger's Syndrome   Learners with Asperger's syndrome can be successfully included in a mainstream classroom, but staff will need some understanding of the specifics of the condition. While many common good practices for all children do apply, there are some specific aspects that will require special understanding and management. Aim – to reduce risk factors by an increase in protective factors through the following.

- Physical arrangements. Allow the learner to sit near to the door and establish a special place in the classroom in order to reduce stress, maybe somewhere the learner can sit and quietly read a book.

- Classroom management. Allow extra time at the end of each lesson/activity for the learner to put books and other equipment away and to get organised for the next lesson or activity.

- Lesson presentation. Wherever possible allow the learner some choice of topic and provide guided notes for activities. Use concrete rather than abstract examples.

- Teaching methods and style. Plan differentiated instructions for the learner – remember instructions and/or explanations may be taken literally. Where possible, devise projects which include hands-on and multisensory tasks. Allow use of the computer to support learning.

- Behavioural management. When faced with problem behaviour, check to make sure it is not a stress reaction. Help the learner to take responsibility for his/her own behavioural choices and to understand the consequences that follow. Aim to be gentle, supportive and creative.

- Teaching behaviours. Give the learner a plan to help make playtimes manageable – where to go and what to do, and how to obtain help. In liaison with home, appoint another learner to be a buddy and offer the buddy appropriate training.

- Specific individual needs. The learner may well find moving between classes difficult and will require support. Places with excessive noise may cause stress in the learner, so teach coping skills, how to avoid such places and relaxation techniques.

- Home–school links. Use a message book and actively involve home in monitoring and supporting learning opportunities in order to develop a team approach.

Remember this is intended as an aide-memoire, with any specific individual there may well be other aspects that will need consideration.

Attention Deficit Hyperactivity Disorder (ADHD)

ADHD is today the most common diagnosis for children who have significant problems in attention, impulsivity and overactivity (3:1 ratio of boys to girls). In the UK, there is a suggestion that the condition is underdiagnosed, with 0.03 per cent of school children being treated with psychostimulants compared to 1 per cent in the US (Holowenko, 1999).

Attention deficit hyperactivity disorder is a pattern of behaviour characterised by three symptoms:

- Inattention – children do not listen to what is said and are easily distracted

- Impulsivity – acting without thinking

- Hyperactivity – being on the go, energetic and haphazard with the potential for frequent accidents.

ADHD is then a medical diagnosis of a behavioural condition which refers to a mixed group of generally disruptive behaviours. Many causes for this condition have been suggested, including minimum brain damage, neurological and/or biochemical as well as genetic neuro dysfunction.

While environmental factors are not implicated in the cause of ADHD, they do have an impact on its course, and ultimate outcome (Holowenko, 1999). For example, having a child with ADHD in the family can disrupt the normal parenting process, but with increased understanding of ADHD some of the more specific problems that learners face are being understood. Dawson and Guare (2004) believe that there is a deficency in a child's executive skills – the higher order cognitive skills which allow us to control and direct our behaviour and include the ability to plan, control negative emotions, such as frustration, and to stay focused on a set task. Learners with ADHD have difficulties in maintaining focused attention on their work, they are easily distracted by peers. For example, goal persistence – the skill of working through sub-goals to achieve a target – is a challenge. Learners will respond to any immediate need, failing to delay it until an appropriate time – they lack what is known as response inhibition. These are higher cognitive skills that most children acquire in the early years. If this is the case, there are implications for how learners with ADHD can be supported effectively through strengthening these skills. Barkley (1997) includes a role for motivation, which can explain why learners have no problems paying attention in one setting, but poor attention in others.

A word of warning at this point. If, under test conditions, a child fails to display a certain problem behaviour, it does not follow that they do not have the problem behaviour in different contexts. Similarly, with learning. Because a child can add numbers to a certain level does not mean that this ability will be readily displayed in the classroom. So much anxiety may be suffered in the situation that this skill is never seen. From this it can be seen that a child with ADHD may not always display some of the common characterisitics but that does not mean that they do not have ADHD. This is very succinctly expressed by Dawson and Guare (2004) as: 'absence of evidence is not evidence of absence'. This may throw light on why a particular tester may comment following observations, 'this child does not have this problem', while the classroom practitioner can also truly say, 'this child *does* have this problem behaviour.' Under test conditions a child may appear not to have the problems over which the school staff are concerned. In reality both are correct, but both need to add, 'under these conditions a child does/does not have ... and can or cannot ...'.

In-class Behaviour Plan for Learners with ADHD   Most learners with ADHD can be effectively supported in mainstream schools. The management approaches recommended are also helpful for the majority of children. Learners with ADHD require the same as most children, only more of it. ADHD is primarily an impairment of a child's ability to regulate behaviour in response to the consequences and rules relating to it. Therefore, any aspect of classroom management regime that seeks to improve this will be a useful strategy. The ideas presented below are intended to explore the key features in the classroom that can make a difference.

Aim – to reduce risk factors by an increase in protective factors through the following.

- Physical arrangements. Allow a quiet work place, with reduced noise and distractions, preferably in clear view of the teacher, but as part of the rest of the class. Use good role models to sit nearby.

- Classroom management. Make sure the learner knows the daily routines, these may be in written or pictorial form. Teach the learner the procedures that underpin the routines and allow for lots of practice. Use frequent rewards with a menu of options for the learner that are presented as soon as possible after the behaviour to reinforce the link between actions and consequences.

- Lesson presentation. When giving the learner instructions maintain eye contact, avoid giving multiple instructions and always check that the learner understands exactly what is expected. For example, teacher asks, 'Do you understand what you are going to do?', pupil responds, 'Yes' (this is not always a true indication). The teacher should ask, 'Tell me briefly what you are going to do first.'

- Teaching methods and style. Break up lessons with different teaching methods – visual, auditory and kinaesthetic – ask the learner for feedback and involve him/her whenever possible.

- Behavioural management. Display the class rules and refer to them often. Work out a rewards plan and have set consequences for learners to make amends for inappropriate behaviours.

- Teaching behaviours. Help the learner to practise such key skills as listening, self-control and friendship-building. Explain the need for the skill, show examples of the skill, set up safe opportunities for them to practise the skill and receive feedback and rewards for their progress.

- Specific individual needs. With the learner develop an individual plan for specific skill weaknesses that he/she needs to develop or strengthen.

- Home–school links. Use a message book and actively involve home in monitoring and supporting learning opportunities relevant to school.

Remember this is intended as an aide-memoire, with any specific individual there may be other aspects that will need consideration.

There are, of course, many more conditions that have social, behavioural and emotional implications for school staff – only the most common have been considered here. When such conditions are medically diagnosed there is, of course, a need for close links being maintained between home, school and other involved professionals. There are, as yet, no cures for these conditions, but the often disabling symptoms can be treated and alleviated. Including learners with these difficulties does not mean that schools should treat them as if they were the same as other learners; rather, inclusion should mean that their unique needs and differences are accepted and responded to positively, appropriately and sensitively.

The MFI (multifaceted intervention) Toolbox, while not designed for these conditions, will contain strategies that could be of value in supporting learners with ADHD or AS, but should only be used in consultation with other professionals involved.

Further Reading 📖

Betts, S., Betts, D. and Gerber-Eckard, L. (2007) *Asperger Syndrome in the Inclusive Classroom: Advice and Strategies for Teachers.* London: Jessica Kingsley.

Furman, B. (2004) *Kids' Skills.* Australia: Innovative Resources.

Holowenko, H. (1999) *Attention Deficit/Hyperactivity Disorder: A Multidisciplinary Approach.* London: Jessica Kingsley.

O'Regan, F. (2007) *Teach and Manage Children with ADHD.* Cambridge: LDA.

Vizard, D. and Vizard, T. (2007) *A Guide to Syndromes and Conditions.* Abbotskerswell, Devon: Behaviour Solutions.

The Toolbox: Dimensions

Children with severe difficulties are clearly recognised and referred on for specialised support. The frustration for school staff can be in supporting those children whose difficulties are not severe enough to be referred on, or if they are referred, rarely, if ever, get to the top of the waiting list. The Toolbox enables staff to systematically work through a problem-solving model, and to then design a support plan for these children.

Understanding a child's behaviour is not easy – no human behaviour is easily understood. All behaviour is multidimensional – that is, there are many causes for the way we are and behave. Psychology has contributed much to our understanding of human behaviour, by breaking down the complex processes into more manageable, understandable parts. Led initially by influential thinkers who, with their followers, developed often unique methods, psychologists were able to develop explanations that focused on specific aspects of human development. The key dimensions and significant contributors are:

- Physiological – Sperry (1951); Selye (1983); Schwartz and Andrasik (2003)

- Feelings – Freud (1930); Adler (1969)

- Behaviour – Pavlov (1927); Watson (1930); Skinner (1971)

- Cognitive – Piaget (1960); Vygotsky (1962); Bruner (1973)

- Social – Sherif (1936); Asch (1955) Milgram (1964); Aronson (1997)

- Happiness – Seligman (2003); Carr (2004a; 2004b); Csikszentmihalyi (1997)

Each of these dimensions has interventions that can be applied to help children and young people cope and manage the challenges they face and will now be considered in more detail.

Physiological

Physiological Dimension

Physiological researchers investigate how the brain and behaviour relate to each other. In the past, the focus was on the structure of the brain, but today, with new technology it is possible to see how the different parts of the brain function. It has been identified that everybody needs a functional level of arousal in the nervous system in order to enable us to meet our daily challenges. With this functional skill we are able to stay focused on a task and ignore distractions. However, if an individual has worries, the amount of brain energy that is available to stay on task is decreased, causing the mind to wander more readily to the areas of concern.

Deep within the brain are structures that are programmed to respond in set ways. This old part of the brain evolved while we were cave and jungle dwellers, therefore the way it learned to respond was adapted to survival in the environment as it was then. The responses triggered are basic in kind, namely: fight, flight, flock, freeze. Evidently these are linked to basic human survival. For example, if we are attacked by a tiger, a very quick burst of energy is required that enables us to move quickly and escape. Thinking about possible responses is not an option and anything that is perceived as a threat needs an immediate response. Notice how any movement just caught at the corner of the eye is distracting, alerting us to possible danger and the need for action.

The connections from the lower brain to the upper 'thinking' brain are very strong, in fact they override what the thinking brain is doing. So, if the lower brain is triggered by a loud noise or sudden movement it will hijack us into action. However, in today's world we are more likely to be threatened as adults by money worries, relationship difficulties or the threat of redundancy rather than imminent attack by a mammoth, but these negative events will still trigger off an instinctual increased arousal level, readying us for action. As a consequence, we are less able to think straight and deal with the everyday tasks at hand. For children, the stresses can include family changes, homework, tests and exams, friendship difficulties or new teachers. These stresses are responded to in the same way as a physical threat. If the individual was about to make a long jump, swim 800 metres or do a BMX stunt, then the tension and increased energy levels would serve a purpose and would be used. But stressed learners can become over-aroused for the task that is challenging them, and can stay tense long after the perceived threat has passed, which is particularly unhelpful. Children can become irritable and apprehensive or develop physical symptoms such as headaches, backaches, digestive and bowel complaints. The state of tension is never fully reduced, so as a result this level of arousal can come to be experienced by the child as the norm. Both parents/carers and teachers can become accustomed to the negative behaviours that are assumed as typical of the child, rather than as symptoms of an underlying state of physical and mental unwellness.

In today's world we do not need much tension and arousal in the nervous system to cope with our daily challenges. Walking and sitting do not require much arousal, but there will be times when an increased level is positive. At exam times, job interviews, impressing a new friend, for example, this arousal can be a motivator – to be at our best.

Being over-aroused can result in exaggerated responses to relatively neutral triggers, so if a child in an already stressed state is presented with new work, there is an increased likelihood that the response will be inappropriate. It is not uncommon for school staff to be surprised by the 'over the top' response that a child or young person has to a simple request. By looking at the situation from a physiological perspective, it becomes more understandable. Many of us will have experienced asking a friend in all innocence, 'How are you today?' only to be faced with floods of tears. Their arousal level is so high that our friend has little or no energy to be brave and natural emotions are displayed.

This dimension of the multifaceted intervention planner is going to be an essential element in helping many of the problems that children face. For example, the explosive child can be taught alternative behaviours, have self-esteem raised, even be taught to recognise and avoid certain triggers, but none of these techniques will be effective unless the child is taught how to control the physiological arousal that tries to hijack them. Furthermore, having learnt a skill is not enough, if that skill is overridden by a basic fight or flight response. This is why children and young people need to learn to control the physiological level of arousal they experience.

The physiologists believed that it was only through an understanding of the 'nuts and bolts' of the system that there could be any understanding of why a behaviour occurred. This can be likened to an understanding of what goes on under the bonnet of a car – knowledge of how the engine works enables the mechanic to fix any faults. Whenever the oldest part of the brain receives messages that suggest danger of some kind it releases hormones into the bloodstream in preparation for action of some kind. The fact that the individual is not being threatened by a tiger but is being called names instead does not matter; the physiological response is the same – preparing for flight or fight. Biologically speaking, survival is what matters, and the nervous system is designed with that in mind. The result is that when young people feel frightened, angry or depressed, the nervous system may respond in less than adaptive ways. While a young person may know the correct response to being teased, the high level of energy in the nervous system prevents rational behaviour, leading possibly to a fight or running away.

Physiological Tools

The physiological dimension offers a range of techniques that will enable young people to learn to stay in control of the symptoms of increased arousal – usually experienced as increased heart rate, faster breathing, perspiration and trembling.

Feelings

Feelings Dimension

Having feelings gives meaning to our lives, from an evolutionary point of view they helped us to survive. Feelings are similar to but different from emotions. Emotion is a much more general term, it describes a complex psychophysical reaction that occurs spontaneously and releases such brain chemicals as adrenalin and cortisol. An emotional reaction is usually to someone or something. Strong emotions will often be physically felt in the body, whereas feelings are what we experience and will be influenced by cognitive and social factors. The basic emotional arousal may be anger, but how we experience it depends on other factors. We 'feel' a different anger in response to a thief who breaks into our home, than to the anger triggered by exploitative practices that defraud people in need. Similarly, we love our favourite holiday destination, but in a different way to the love we have for our partner. Using feelings can be a way of understanding the many subjective experiences, positive or negative, that learners have in schools.

Learners who face such challenges as communication and learning difficulties, visual and/or auditory impairments and physical and/or medical disabilities are especially vulnerable to experiencing negative feelings. Each of these challenges involves children experiencing a sense of loss in being different from other children. There are many emotional reactions to loss including: anger, sadness, fear, shame, embarrassment. Many of the children who need support are likely to be coping with a range of these negative emotions, some of which will be suppressed. When emotions are bottled up, for whatever reason, the energy will still need to be released in some way. This is when surface behavioural difficulties are often observed that in reality mask underlying emotional knots.

Understanding emotions has become of central importance in all schools. 'Emotional intelligence' and 'emotional literacy' are concepts that are shaping new initiatives in schools today. The work of Daniel Goleman has raised awareness of the importance of emotions in learning. Learning is both a social and emotional experience and Goleman (1995) has popularised the concept of emotional intelligence. This involves the innate ability to feel emotions, to remember them and to communicate them. Emotional intelligence and emotional literacy merge into each other. Emotional literacy is concerned with the ability to express feelings and to manage such negative feelings as anger. It is, therefore, understandable why emotional literacy especially has been embraced within education when it is often the children who lack these skills that cause themselves and others distress. Today, we appreciate that there are children who leave school with a lower self-esteem than when they started because children with a low self-esteem tend to try less, consequently succeed less, naturally fuelling their feelings of low self-worth. It takes confidence for a learner to risk attempting new tasks, therefore negative feelings, such as anxiety, fear and depression, will interfere with a young person's ability to engage with new learning challenges. Learning is in fact an emotional experience just as much as a thinking one.

Feelings tools

Tools that will be developed for this dimension will include a focus on interventions to deal with negative emotions as well as raising a learner's sense of

Feelings

personal confidence. This is such a wide area that it is impossible to detail all the possible emotions that may be involved in any problem. Therefore, intervention techniques for the most common emotional difficulties, namely low self-esteem, frustration and anger, will be considered.

Self-esteem

Self-esteem is so central to supporting learners who face SEBD that it will be given special consideration.

The life experiences children have influence how they respond to their world and how they come to regard themselves within that world. Children who face SEBD are at a greater risk of an emotionally negative self-concept.

Self-esteem is one of the most important, yet elusive concepts in education. While it concerns an individual's feelings of self, it is also strongly influenced by the behaviour of others, especially during early childhood. Research shows that even in the playgroup preschoolers respond differently to those peers they detect as 'being different':

> Pre-schoolers behave as if they know who talks well and who does not, and they prefer to interact with those who do. (Hadley and Rice, 1991)

Why is Self-esteem so Important? For many educators self-esteem is the most important factor in a learner's success – 'children learn well with a combination of appropriately high expectations and appropriately high self-esteem' (Roberts, 2002). In school, learners need to be able to take risks in order to learn. Learning new tasks almost inevitably involves some failure at some time but it is the ability to cope with the ensuing frustration that takes a degree of confidence, which some learners do not have. They are so worried about failing that they prefer not to attempt the new task, thereby protecting the little self-esteem they possess.

Low self-esteem is associated with many childhood disorders. It seems reasonable to argue that those children with a positive self-esteem are able to cope more effectively with some of the challenges they face. If you are physically run-down then you are more susceptible to illnesses, similarly, a lack of self-confidence and self-belief leaves an individual more prone to psychological disorders.

The relationship between academic achievement and self-esteem remains confusing. Does a good self-esteem increase achievement or does achievement raise self-esteem? It seems to be a 'chicken and egg' question. The truth is probably that the influence is in both directions. It is known that children who believe in their abilities tend to achieve more, therefore, a 'self-fulfilling prophecy' could be at work.

The adult that we each become is shaped by the input we received as a child – the better the input, the better the output. Just as a child will not grow into a physically healthy adult if they lack the right vitamins in childhood, similarly, their emotional nourishment will be lacking if they have not been praised and helped to support themselves.

Key Terms Some key terms within this area include – self-concept, ideal self, self-esteem and global self-esteem.

Self-concept is the perception the child has of himself. The ways in which he defines himself. For example, 'I am a boy', 'I am Ken's best friend', 'I play football', 'I enjoy cartoons'. These are all individual components that go towards making up the person.

Ideal self is the kind of person an individual would ideally like to be. In children this will often be in comparison to other children. Some examples could be: 'I would like to be popular with my friends', 'I would like my hair to be straighter', 'I would like to have a boyfriend'. Self-esteem is the evaluation of those parts: 'How much do I value being Ken's friend?', 'How important is having a boyfriend?'

A child's self-esteem is then a combination of objective information about oneself and a subjective evaluation of that information. It is the gap between how individual children see themselves and how they would like to be, that gives them their self-esteem. There will be specific areas where a learner's self-esteem may be high or low, possibly being good at art, but poor at spelling, but all of these different aspects combine to give an individual what is known as global self-esteem.

Global self-esteem is the overall state of feeling that we have towards ourselves. There will be specific areas where we feel good about ourselves and others which are not so positive.

While there are many causes for a low self-esteem, in school we need to be aware that:

- Distorted self-evaluation can cause a low self-esteem. Some children can be driven by a perfectionist nature to try to achieve beyond their abilities.

- Being teased or bullied by peers is a serious at-risk experience. The importance of children's peers in the development of a healthy sense of identity cannot be underestimated. This is why bullying is such a serious cause for concern.

Other reasons include, children who have experienced attachment difficulties with their carers as well as those children who have a strong inferiority complex. Sometimes children can be successful learners but negatively judge themselves in comparison with others. Alternatively, a learner may lack certain skills, for example, singing or playing football, but overrate the importance of those skills. For some children a low self-esteem will be the result of a poor ability to communicate through speech and language difficulties, and this will effectively limit the success of their social interactions.

Experiencing a low self-esteem at some time is normal. We all sometimes fall below our personal expectations, or the expectations of those who are important to us. We typically work through this dip, we learn new skills and change our expectations. A low self-esteem is not a problem in itself, providing we have a reservoir of good feelings towards ourselves in order to help heal ourselves.

Age differences and self-esteem   Achieving reliable measures of a child's self-esteem is a difficult task – younger children are more prone to act out their feelings, whereas older ones tend to mask their inner feelings. The variation between children of different ages is obvious. Below are some general guidelines to consider when working with those in early childhood as compared to late childhood. The practitioner should always bear in mind that generalities do not necessarily apply to any particular instance. Just because most older children are better able to verbalise their feelings, it does not follow that this is necessarily true for the individual child with whom you are working.

Younger children (primary age)

'Acting out' behaviours may reflect negative feelings

Enjoy concrete activities – games etc.

The problem behaviour is situation specific.

Personality traits are less consistent.

Have a limited vocabulary.

Older children (secondary age)

Have increased self-awareness.

Have a wider emotional vocabulary.

Are likely to reflect negative emotions in 'acting out'.

Are prone to give socially desirable answers.

Show negative emotions through sadness, isolation and passivity.

Their low self-esteem is more pervasive across situations.

Frustration

Turning to consider the second most common emotional difficulty. All learners will face some frustration at times as they learn new skills. Frustration in this context can be defined as the state of raised emotional and physiological arousal that occurs when a desired goal is not achieved through a lack of the necessary skills. Children have within them the capacity to develop skills that are especially important in the classroom. These are often referred to as executive skills or higher cognitive abilities, some of which are:

- self-regulation of feelings
- task initiation
- goal-directed persistence
- planning
- sustained attention.

The skill that concerns us most is the self-regulation of emotions, or 'frustration control'. This is a learner's ability to manage personal frustration and stay on task, despite immediate failure. The build up of frustration can often result in either tears or aggressive outbursts. The reasons why some children fail to develop the skill of frustration control may include:

- attention deficit disorder

- neurological damage

- learning difficulties

- parenting style

- acute anxiety.

In some children several of these conditions may combine to reduce a young person's ability to tolerate emotional distress.

 Case Study 3.1

John is in Year 5 and has a history of losing control when faced with new work. At first he makes a definite effort to do the new task on his own, and with some adult support will make progress, but support staff describe his behaviour as being 'panic like' – starting to breathe fast and with his muscles visibly tensing up. No matter how much encouragement he is given, he starts to cry and will try to leave the classroom. Through examining techniques available within the Toolbox school staff involved could begin to address these issues and help John control his frustration.

Anger

The third common emotion is anger. Children will feel anger for many reasons but interventions to be suggested are for those children who have not learnt the skills of expressing or controlling anger in socially acceptable ways. This is very different from those children whose anger stems, for example, from having been abused, neglected or for those who are suffering bereavement.

Anger is a normal emotion that all children experience. It is a state of physiological arousal that provides us with the energy to overcome dangers and obstacles that threaten us. Anger in itself is not the problem, it is how it is expressed. For example, when a child is not being allowed to have a certain toy 'now' and hits the child who has it out of frustration, then the aggressive outburst is the problem.

The learner who is frequently angry and aggressive is often:

- unaware of how his behaviour affects others

- lacks the appropriate skills to meet his needs

- is often impulsive.

Feelings

So anger can be defined as having the following features:

- It is a feeling. There is a physiological component to it, and this aims to prepare the individual for some kind of action.

- It usually occurs in response to something that has happened.

- It is often visible through aggressive actions, but it does not always lead to aggression.

Children that experience difficulties in anger control frequently blame others for their feelings and behaviour. They externalise the causes of their own behaviour, for example, 'He wound me up'. It is not uncommon for them to be involved in bullying and vandalism (Nicolson and Ayers, 2004).

In peer relationships the child who cannot control their anger can make matters progress from bad to worse. For example, if John feels frustrated because he is not invited to play with other children, he may approach the others in a threatening and pushy manner. The other children become apprehensive and frightened, and reject any of John's approaches. This makes John more angry and his behaviour even more threatening, thereby reducing the chances of him being allowed to join in the group even further – creating a vicious circle of anger and rejection.

Feeling Tools

Each of these three emotional difficulties, namely low self-esteem, frustration and anger, will have tools that can enable a learner to either cope with them or learn to express/manage them in more effective ways. It follows that the level of understanding a learner has will determine the choice of intervention.

Behaviour

Behaviour Dimension

A group of psychologists known as the behaviourists refused to study what could not be seen, such as thoughts and emotions. Instead they attempted to make psychology a science, based on evidence and facts, not intuitions and conjectures. They aimed to show that by studying what happened before and after an action, sense could be made of the reasons behind the behaviour. For example, if a child receives praise for doing a piece of work, then the likelihood of that behaviour happening again is increased. It is what a specific behaviour earns that either increases or decreases the reoccurrence of that behaviour:

> If a certain behaviour increases in frequency because it is followed by positive consequences, or is not followed by negative consequences, then that behaviour has been reinforced. (Stallard, 2002: 2)

The power of contingencies on human behaviour should never be underestimated. The founder of behaviourism, J.B. Watson, stated:

> Give me a dozen healthy infants, well-formed, and my own special world to bring them up in, and I'll guarantee to take any one at random and train him to become any type of specialist, I might select doctor, lawyer, artist, merchant chief, and, yes, beggarman and thief. (Watson, 1930: 104)

The behaviourists observed that more often we tend to do those things that obtain something we like, and less often those things that are followed by unpleasant consequences. Understanding these principles can help us avoid making behavioural mistakes, for example, if a pupil learns that misbehaving results in exclusion from a lesson they didn't like, then they are likely to misbehave more often. Behaviour, then, is greatly influenced by environmental factors and there are triggers that cue certain behaviours in certain places. Learners learn to adapt their behaviours depending on the subject being taught, how it is taught and who is teaching it. What follows the specific behaviour then reinforces it in some manner and learners develop behavioural pathways that serve a function for them. The tools that will be developed here are based on a rigorous and scientific approach, the techniques are based on direct observation of how environmental factors affect a learner's behaviour. This approach believes that human behaviour is cued by factors in the environment – antecedents or triggers that cue the behaviour – and are maintained by the consequences that follow the behaviour. The triggers may be a combination of distal, or distant triggers, and proximal – close and immediate ones. Two examples follow to illustrate this.

 Case Study 3.2   Mark, who has learning and communication difficulties

Distal Factors

These difficulties are the distal antecedents – they are important for school staff to know, they will influence how staff relate to and teach him. They are the setting conditions that help us understand Mark better.

Proximal Factors

In school, Mark's problem behaviours are often triggered when he is presented with structured work that is beyond his ability. By exploring Mark's situation in more detail, it can be observed that when Mark shouts out, disturbs his peers and bangs his desk, his teacher and support staff give him a verbal warning to stop. As a result, Mark receives negative attention from adults as well as attention from his peers and he avoids doing the work. Negative attention is more acceptable to Mark than no attention at all so his behaviour is maintained by the consequences. The immediate proximal antecedent, or trigger for the behaviour, is the type of work Mark is expected to do

 ### Case Study 3.3   Sasha, whose home circumstances have changed

Distal Factors

The school Education Welfare Officer has found that Sasha's home circumstances are very distressing. Her parents are separating and her mother, with whom Sasha lives, is seriously ill. School cannot change these sad events, but an understanding can help them make sense of Sasha's difficult behaviours.

Proximal Factors

In class, Sasha's behaviour deteriorates when she is expected to engage in cooperative group work. Her behaviour is negative and she often torments her peers until an argument starts, therefore few of her peers are ever happy to work with her.

A pathway can be seen to Sasha's behaviour. When working with peers, her need seems to be to hurt them. It is not usual for happy well-balanced children to regularly hurt others, but if a child is hurting inside, then the type of behaviour that Sasha displays is more likely to occur. Her negative, spiteful behaviour can be seen to be driven by her own internal painful feelings that are a reflection of her home life.

There are three core assumptions that underpin this behavioural approach. Frequently occurring problem behaviours are:

- predictable – there are cues to them
- functional – something is obtained that the individual would like to achieve now and/or in the future, therefore there is a purpose
- changeable – new ways of responding can be taught and learned.

This approach is typically used when there is an excess of a certain behaviour (for example, shouting out, disturbing others), or if there is a deficit of a behaviour (for example, a child rarely interacting with other children). It is the excessive behaviours that demand most attention because they usually directly affect adults and other children. Often punitive techniques are applied to extinguish the behaviour but sadly

Behaviour

many children habituate to constant negative feedback – being told off, detentions, etc. As a result, adults who rely heavily on this approach become more frustrated and stressed because what should work, is not working. Usually, it is always the same small group of children and young people who are given sanctions. In most schools it is approximately 5 per cent of the children who are responsible for over 50 per cent of the discipline referrals (Crone and Horner, 2003).

The application of positive reinforcement techniques has been found to be more effective and less stressful. To increase the behaviours that we wish to see more often means that we use support and encouragement instead of trying to reduce inappropriate behaviours by the use of negative techniques and punishments. In all relationships such negative techniques are harmful and damaging, and can also increase the likelihood of more negative behaviour given the norm of reciprocity, that is, 'You get what you give'. Also, as educationalists, our aim should be to increase a child's behavioural repertoire, increasing the choices in behavioural options available, rather than reducing them

Behavioural tools

Behavioural tools focus on how the environment relates to behaviour. Using tools to alter either the triggers to behaviour or the consequences that follow allow changes to be made.

Cognitive Dimension

A different approach was taken by the cognitivists, who said that while thoughts were not easy to study they could not be ignored:

> the way a stimulus is processed mentally through perceiving, attending, thinking, expecting, remembering, and analysing is at least as important in determining a behavioural response as the stimulus itself, if not more so. (Hock, 2005: 114)

Through language it is possible for individuals to solve problems, communicate complex ideas and, through thoughts and beliefs, shape the way we react to our world. Our problems are in part caused by the way we think about them. If a child believes they are 'stupid', then whether it is true or not, they act as if it were, thereby turning it into a truth.

The ability to solve problems is a skill that has enabled us to survive in the most inhospitable places on earth. Using language we are able to imagine and verbalise all kinds of possibilities before they exist. Children are natural thinkers – they do not need to teach their digestive systems to digest food, similarly, they do not need to teach their brains to process information – it happens naturally. How children think about themselves, consciously and unconsciously, will influence how they feel and behave. A learner who has a positive attitude towards making mistakes will make much more progress than the one who fears making mistakes. In the early years children develop thinking styles that can help or hinder later learning. The school staff who reward a learner for mastering new words are doing something important, but if they also have the skill to develop a positive attitude in the child towards learning, then they will have made an even bigger difference.

Children with learning difficulties are especially at risk of holding negative attitudes towards learning. They will often have a poor sense of personal worth. Many children learn that to be valued is to be clever because they live in a learning environment that tests them for their successes – not their efforts, determination and enjoyment. For those with learning difficulties it is hardly surprising that they come to see themselves as less valued than those who are successful learners.

These children can become reluctant and resistant primary school learners, and disaffected and disengaged secondary school learners. Why should they take part in a competition in which they only experience failure? School staff notice that these children often shy away from praise – no matter how small the task is made to ensure success, they still seem reluctant to try.

> Discouraged children, trapped in a self-concept created by past experiences of failure, will lose out in a particularly disheartening way when a praising teacher fails to understand, and thus to address, the effects of such painful experiences on their low self-image as learners. Consequently, a praise refusing student's determination not to be lured into the risks of failing yet again may be further reinforced. (Hanko, 1994: 166)

A child's thoughts and beliefs need to be addressed as much as self-esteem and behaviour as all of these components interact with each other. Expecting to fail can lead to failure; lacking confidence can lead to failure. Negative thoughts and beliefs effect what a child does and feels. A child who faces learning difficulties is at risk of developing such core beliefs as: 'I always get things wrong', 'I'm not as clever as others', 'I can't organise myself', 'I am not as valued as others'. These core beliefs, formed through early learning experiences, can give rise to a constant stream of what are known as 'automatic thoughts'. These thoughts influence feelings of self and what an individual then does. (It should be stressed that our core beliefs are usually a mixture of both positive and negative.)

Beliefs such as these make assumptions about how we will respond in new situations and from these subconscious beliefs come conscious automatic thoughts. Picture the mind as if it was an iceberg, with conscious thoughts that we are aware of being the tip of the iceberg above water, while below the surface are many beliefs about ourselves and other people. These 'under the surface' beliefs are triggered by specific events, for example, a new learning challenge that throws up into conscious awareness automatic interpretations of what is going to happen. The individual can hear these interpretations often, so is familiar with them, and the more they are heard, the more they are believed. If a child has mainly negative interpretations of what is going to happen then this can lead to negative behaviour. For example, if the child has the thought that 'I will mess up in this test', then it is likely that he will try less hard and prepare less than he should. Therefore, when he does mess up, he just confirms the belief that he had about himself in the first place.

Cognitive Tools

This dimension will provide many interventions. This is the one area where a learner's awareness and understanding of the difficulties to be faced can be central to helping behavioural change. At a surface level, learners can be helped to self-monitor their own behaviour and often once behaviour is closely monitored, it will change merely through that process. At a deeper level, techniques will need to be developed that can help a learner challenge deeply held, but erroneous, self-beliefs. For example, many learners have a core belief that they are stupid or unlikeable but such irrational beliefs can be challenged and restructured. Techniques developed here are not quick fixes, but essential for any long-term change. Cognitive restructuring techniques aim to challenge negative and faulty thinking over a period of time.

Social Dimension

We all live in groups of some kind, whether it is family, friendship groups, school class, religious or political party, we are fundamentally social animals and we seek the company of others –

> the first evidence of his inborn social feeling unfolds in his early search for affection, which leads him to seek the proximity of adults. (Adler, 1992: 46)

It is not uncommon for school staff to experience a very likeable child on a one-to-one basis, but when the child is in class, working in the company of peers, staff can experience a different individual. The social dimension to behaviour cannot be ignored. Sometimes children fail to acquire good friendship skills and their time in school can be a negative experience as a result.

Being social animals we have developed complex rules as to how to behave in different social contexts. Being a member of a group satisfies a basic human need to belong and as a group member there is the need to feel valued and to have some influence or power – being a part of a school class is no different. Children naturally make behavioural mistakes as they learn how to meet such key needs as obtaining attention, being valued and having some influence in a class situation. Therefore, in school it is a common observation that a learner can be well behaved in some lessons, but can be disruptive in other classes. Also children rarely use the language that they use with friends at home – they have been socialised into the appropriate behaviour for the appropriate situation. For some children, succeeding at being a group member is one of the most challenging aspects of school life. As children grow older it is their peers who become most important to them. Therefore, one of the most significant groups that children are allocated to during their childhood is their school class – many of them mixing with the same peers in school for possibly 11 or more years, with the result that often long-lasting friendships are formed with some of these peers. Children learn about themselves by comparing themselves to others, but for many children, some of the time, school experiences can be both challenging and stressful.

For example, children with learning or communication difficulties will compare themselves with peers who do not have such challenges. Such skills are key to being successful in today's learning environment and children quickly learn that the dominant value in school is success. To be successful is to be valued, but those with pre-emptive barriers to success face the risk of devaluing themselves. How a child reacts to and copes with feeling different to the majority of his or her peers will depend on many factors including personality, family background, self-worth, etc. But it is reasonable to say that some of the problem behaviour that is observed in the group context is a response to the way in which schools have been organised and established, with a set curriculum that all children must either follow or aim to achieve at some level.

There will also be children who lack the social interactional skills that are necessary to become a group member, including the skills of sharing, turn-taking, listening and conflict resolution which are often taken for granted. It is assumed that children will have acquired these skills in their early years from their family but that is not necessarily the case. This is an assumption that schools are beginning to, and need to, question. In order for children to learn collaboratively then these skills, which are essential, will need to be actively taught to some. If the lack of these skills is not addressed then the problem behaviours that distract teachers from teaching and children learning will persist. When looking at the problem profile of some children it will become clear that core interventions will arise from this social dimension.

Having the necessary skills to cooperate, and to generally be a team player are fundamental for all children to be happy and successfully included into their peer group. Children with social skill deficits are likely to be excluded from friendship groups at an early age, and by secondary age it is often observed that those with poor social skills seem to band together (thereby becoming the worst of possible role models for one another.)

A key skill that is fundamental to developing successful interactional skills is the ability to predict. By learning what to expect in a given situation, the world becomes a safer place, while the unpredictable can be unsettling. Once a child can trust another child not hurt or threaten him/her, then a secure friendship can develop, but if a child has social skill deficits this can negatively affect relationships with peers. For example, if a child is volatile and quick tempered, then other children become wary of efforts to befriend or play.

What is it that enables children to be skilled and adaptive in this area? The skills needed are both complex and interrelated, and show a growing child's ability to plan ahead. As Ladd and Mize (1983) explain:

> They are able to organise cognitions and behaviours into an effective course of action to reach culturally acceptable interpersonal goals, and to evaluate and change goal-directed behaviour continuously to maximise their chances of achieving such goals. (Ladd and Mize, 1983: 154)

Our aim is to support those learners who face relationship difficulties because of deficits in their social skills repertoire.

Social Tools

Usually children learn the necessary social skills for the many different contexts in which they live, such as how to behave at home with their family, with relatives, friends on the street, in the playground and the classroom. Children rarely use the same language at home as they do with their friends – each situation has slightly different norms which govern what is considered the correct behaviour. Children usually learn through imitating others, having the right behaviour encouraged and the wrong behaviour discouraged, but for some children this is not sufficient for them to master the necessary skills, they will need more formal instruction. Social skills training tools help learners acquire the necessary skills. Instead of being punished for not behaving appropriately, they can be taught to improve more appropriate behaviour, while seeing 'behavioural mistakes as learning opportunities'.

Happiness Dimension

A section on happiness may be a surprise as we so often take this state of mind for granted and consequently ignore the skills that are required to maintain it. We all want children to have happy childhoods, and the majority do, being robust and resilient to the everyday knocks of life. However, sadly there are a significant number of children who are less likely to enjoy their school years. Some of these children will come from families where there are at-risk factors that have a negative influence on their development, but there will be others who may be happy at home, but lack friends in school, or struggle with their work.

By walking in their shoes for a day, we would be better placed to understand why children with SEBD behave as they do and why happiness can seem an unattainable concept for them. Can we imagine the stress a child feels when their family is falling apart? How would you feel in lessons when the work is beyond you? How would you cope with the frustration of not been able to fully express your needs or understand the many messages you receive each day? Could you cope with struggling to do what your peers do naturally, for example, reading or catching a ball? Or what about not being able to see or hear clearly the instructions that are presented to you? Can you imagine what it would feel like just not being able to keep up and be the same as your peers? As Charles Dickens said, 'it was the best of times, it was the worst of times' (1859).

In the past, the aim of psychologists and other practitioners was to reduce pain and suffering, and through the years much progress has been achieved in this area. Yet despite increased economic prosperity, negative indicators such as childhood psychopathological disorders – including depression, eating disorders, and self-harm – seem to relentlessly increase (Rutter and Smith, 1995). This led to a new movement known as Positive Psychology (Carr, 2004b), that focuses on increasing children's and adults' sense of well-being and happiness. While everyone may have a biologically set range in which to experience happiness, there are skills that can be applied to support this state. For example, in a race the winner of the bronze medal may be happier than the person who won silver; the reason being that the bronze winner is just happy to be on the medal podium, while the silver winner may feel disappointed that the gold was just out of reach. One has the skill of enjoying what they have whilst the other bemoans what wasn't to be.

There can be an assumption that if a problem is removed for a child, then there will automatically be an increased feeling of happiness and well-being. This is not necessarily true. If a child has been trapped in negativity for some time by a problem behaviour or feeling, then he is likely to need help to enjoy himself and feel happy again. When the problem behaviour is removed there can be an assumption that a child is permanently 'cured' and happy, but if new setbacks occur, as they inevitably do, there can be a serious risk of relapse to the original state of problem behaviour. This also applies to adults who suffer from depression, even though the depression may seem to have been dealt with and cured, often through medication. When future difficulties have to be faced, a relapse into the same old familiar problem behaviours can occur. Children who have experienced negative thoughts, feelings and behaviours need to develop and learn coping methods to increase their happiness. The existing formalised education system sets a range of requirements

Happiness

and standards which some learners will struggle to meet – the consequences of failing to meet these demands can result in serious damage to personal happiness.

Before attempting to define the elusive concept of happiness, the following factors seem to make a contribution.

- Genetics. Each person appears to be equipped with a set range within which happiness occurs, given through our biological inheritance. There may be periods when this range is exceeded but the tendency will be to pull us back into our norm. Seligman (2003) quotes the case of a sad and lonely woman who won a lottery of approximately six million pounds. After a peak period of elation she returned to the same degree of unhappiness as she had before – even though she was now considerably wealthier. Her situation had vastly improved but her mindset was the same. Sceptics may argue that she obviously wasn't spending her money on the right things!

- Circumstances. There are known social circumstances that seem to correlate with happiness – including friendships, marital state, religion, education and money.

- Personal factors. This is the most important aspect, as it refers to those factors over which we can exert some control. 'It is not things themselves that disturb us but the view we take of them' (Epitectus).

The attitude taken to events that happen in life is a key determining factor in the level of happiness that individuals experience. It is well known that many learners are held back, not by their general or specific learning difficulties, but by their attitude – 'I just can't do it'.

An individual's attitude to life is often summed up as being either optimistic or pessimistic – seemingly two stable personality traits. How we regard yesterday and what we plan for tomorrow will be greatly determined by the attitudinal framework through which we perceive them. Early experiences help shape the deep-seated thoughts that are held by individuals. Many conscious thoughts are influenced by beliefs that are so much a part of us that we are unaware of them.

What is happiness?

It is a term used in so many different ways, to mean so many different things, that the task of defining happiness has defeated many of our greatest thinkers. No word can be easy to define when the following sentence makes sense:

'You are leaving to start work in another school and that makes me unhappy. But I am really happy that you have found the right school where you can further your career.'

There is a danger of being drawn into the type of linguistic debates that Humpty Dumpty had:

'When I use a word,' Humpty Dumpty said, in rather a scornful tone, 'it means just what I choose it to mean – neither more nor less.'

'The question is,' said Alice, 'whether you *can* make words mean so many different things.'

Happiness

'The question is,' said Humpty Dumpty, 'which is to be master – that's all.' (Lewis Carroll, 2005 [1872]: 80)

One person's happiness can be another's displeasure. Trying to define the word 'yellow' can be a similar problem.

I don't know if you see the same yellow as me, but I do know that when I say please pass the yellow cup, you pass the cup that I expected. (Gilbert, 2006)

So perhaps a functional pragmatic definition will have to suffice. For us, happiness is an emotional state that is pleasing and motivates us to repeat it and it can be caused by many circumstances.

People from the same culture, living at the same time, tend towards similar events that give rise to what is commonly called 'happiness'. People living 200 years ago would in all probability have had a different definition as to what made them happy.

Happiness does seem to have two key elements. First, there is a definite 'feeling' side to it – happiness means the presence of pleasure, doing something we enjoy and avoiding displeasure or those things that hurt or upset. Second, happiness also involves, 'thinking'. That is, a person reflects and thinks about what has taken place, giving rise to a sense of satisfaction in what has been achieved.

Happiness 'depends both on feeling (pleasure and displeasure) and thinking (satisfaction); it involves both the heart and the head' (Martin, 2006: 16). A view supported by Thomas Jefferson, who wrote, 'happiness is not being pained in body or troubled in mind' (Brallier and Chabert, 1996: 21).

It follows then that a person can be happy while not actually experiencing pleasure, for example, when a good deed is recalled that was carried out last week creating feelings of satisfaction and happiness. This is a different aspect of happiness compared to the feelings experienced, for example, when buying a longed-for iPod or new electronic game.

Today, in our commercially dominated world, it is more often feelings of pleasure obtained from material objects that dominate. The immediate pleasure experienced from food, television, toys, clothes, etc. is a 'quick fix' for feeling good. Happiness dependent on feelings can lead to an overdependence on material things, and the happiness derived from pleasurable experiences tends to be short lived.

The important nature and place of happiness in schools is more fully recognised today. The Social Emotional Aspects of Learning (SEAL) Primary National Strategy clearly states that a key aim for children is to:

explore feelings of happiness and excitement, sadness, anxiety and fearfulness, while learning (and putting into practice) shared models for 'calming down' and 'problem solving'. (DfES, 2005)

An increased understanding of happiness will enable practitioners to construct a range of interventions to raise the spirits of those children and young people who

Happiness

have faced negative inputs, that is, poor relationships with peers, adults and/or themselves. Research (Carr, 2004b) suggests that happiness involves the following components:

- Relationships: Having the skills to relate positively and to feel part of a group is a strong source of well-being, this enables a child to engage in shared activities and hobbies.

- Environment: Attending a school that feels safe and caring, where learning is undertaken in an emotionally secure manner, all helps children to feel happy. Having classrooms that are bright and stimulating, playgrounds with gardens etc. all serve to contribute to a child's well-being. The physical environment raises or depresses spirits – obscene graffiti, abandoned cars, etc. do have a negative effect.

- Physical health: Encouraging children to eat a healthy diet and to exercise is part of feeling good.

- Competency: Children are naturally programmed to develop core skills, through play and work. There is an enjoyment in learning to ride a bike, catch a ball, read a book, solve sums, etc.

- Leisure: Being able to relax and unwind, taking part in recreational activities, clubs, etc.

- Comparisons: Children with specific difficulties can be trapped into comparing themselves to inappropriate reference groups. There is a strong need in educational settings to establish fair and reasonable reference groups. To not address this issue is to cultivate the ground for low self-esteem in many learners.

Boosting Positive Emotions

It is generally agreed that negative emotions increase the likelihood of even more negative emotions. If an individual feels depressed there is an inherent logic in feeding this depression by not going out, letting personal care slip, avoiding new challenges. All of these activities feed negative emotions and a sense of spiralling downwards. Reversely, there is also a positive spiral where positive feelings increase the likelihood of more positive ones:

> positive emotion leads to exploration, which leads to mastery and mastery leads not only to more positive emotion but to the discovery of your child's signature strengths. (Seligman, 2003: 231)

Therefore, the positive feelings children and young people have in school should be taken as seriously as their negative ones. Positive feelings help children to recognise their abilities and talents as well as to be curious and adventurous intellectually and socially. Meeting new learning challenges takes courage and confidence, positive feelings in schools are not an optional extra, they are essential for a child to risk learning. The negative emotions of fear and anxiety lead a child to withdraw, close down and self-protect because of feeling under attack.

Happiness does not come automatically, it is not a gift that good fortune bestows upon certain people and a reversal of fortune takes back, it depends on the individual alone. One does not become happy overnight, but with patient labour, day after day. Happiness is constructed, and that requires effort and time. In order to become happy, we have to learn how to change ourselves.

Happiness Tools

The tools that will be considered are not based on wishful thinking or dubious research, but are based on a new scientific study of happiness known as Positive Psychology. A major contributor and advocate of this approach is Martin Seligman, professor of psychology and ex-president of the American Psychological Association, whose work provides a range of validated techniques to teach those children and young people who have faced adversity of one kind or another how to be happy. The techniques advocated are good for all children, but it is accepted that most children grow in emotionally secure, caring relationships that make them less necessary.

If happiness is viewed as a skill there are specific techniques that can increase a child's sense of well-being. These skills can help children face the challenges they will meet and can be taught and practised as ways to lift their spirits as well as being applied proactively for all. An example skill is that of 'signature strengths'. All children have a skill or attribute at which they are good – possibly sport, singing, writing or helping others. Finding opportunities for children to use their own signature strength is a sure way to increase their sense of personal value and happiness. Investigating happiness gives rise to the challenge of considering whether it might be possible to help troubled children live happier lives.

The Compartments of the Toolbox

The temptation for the practitioner is that any of the above approaches could be used exclusively in isolation, but the fact is that they all contribute towards a greater understanding of what it is to be human. To ignore any of them lessens our understanding of and ability to actively help those children who require extra support.

For example, raising the self-esteem of a child who has dyslexia is important but is it enough for him just to feel better about himself? A change in the child's thinking from 'I am not as clever as others' to 'I'm not such a good reader as Mary, but my reading is improving and I'm much better at it' is a good start. However, deeply held beliefs that are well established and familiar are not easily changed. It will take some focused assistance to enable this pupil to challenge old ways and learn new ways of thinking. So raising a learner's self-esteem is important, but is not enough – the challenge is to work at a number of levels and aspects of his behaviour.

Using the MFI Toolbox

The core assumption to this approach is that all children's SEBD are multifaceted, and multifaceted problems need multifaceted solutions. The following example shows the toolbox approach in action.

 Case Study 3.4   Jane, 10 years old

In school Jane, who is 10 years old, is of concern to her class teacher. Jane will rarely volunteer any information in class and behaves in a passive and withdrawn manner. Her teacher and classroom assistant describe Jane as having a worrying lack of self-esteem. During playtimes Jane is more often found with the supervisor than playing with friends and it is not unusual for Jane to complain that 'No one wants to play with me'. When interviewed, Jane talks of feeling lonely and isolated and thinks that no one likes her. She explains that whenever she tries to join in with other children it makes no difference: 'They seem to just ignore me. I end up feeling even more stupid and anxious.'

Applying the MFI Toolbox

The pen picture of Jane's difficulties illustrates there are several aspects to them. Possible areas for concerns include:

- a negative thinking style
- poor friendship skills
- anxiety being displayed as a stress indicator.

It can be seen that Jane's difficulties have several dimensions that need to be addressed.

A key member of staff who knows Jane well completes the questionnaire section of the Toolbox, which takes approximately 15 minutes. There are a set of 'indicative' questions for each of the six dimensions. There are 10 questions to each dimension (but just three questions are used here as examples). The completed questionnaire then forms the basis for a profile of the problem and indicates the core dimensions that require interventions.

Physiological dimension – example indicative questions

- Does the learner show facial colour changes – flushed or pale – in certain situations?
- Does the learner seem hesitant and anxious?
- Does the the learner seem to lack energy and motivation?

Feelings dimension – example indicative questions

- Does the learner's body posture/s suggest negative feelings?
- Does the learner show little pleasure in specific activities?
- Is the learner unable to empathise with peers?

Behavioural dimension – example indicative questions

- Do there seem to be definite identifiable triggers to the learner's behaviour?
- Are there predictable consequences to the learner's behaviour?
- Can you identify rewards that the learner enjoys and seeks?

Cognitive dimension – example indicative questions

- Does the learner explain her failures in terms of a lack of ability?
- Does the learner compare herself to peers, 'I'm not as clever as them'?
- Does the learner believe that she is unpopular with her peers, 'No one likes me'?

Social dimension – example indicative questions

- Does the learner have difficulties interacting with peers?
- Does the learner spend time with older or younger children?
- Does the learner have more problem behaviour during playtimes?

Happiness dimension – example indicative questions

- Does the learner find it difficult to readily recall happy memories?
- Does the learner find adapting to normal changes, for example, new staff, difficult?
- Does the learner have little awareness of her personal uniqueness, value and strengths?

After completing the questionnaire it was decided that Jane could be helped in the following areas with these tools. (The full details of each of these tools and how they can be used is provided in Chapter 5.)

(Continued)

(Continued)

Interventions

- Physiological tools: Specific relaxation techniques to help Jane manage her anxiety.

- Thinking tools: Positive thinking techniques to help Jane challenge her persisitent negative interpretation of events involving her.

- Social tools: Friendship skills training to improve her peer relationships.

- Happiness tools: Developing a programme to build on one of Jane's strengths – she is a good singer – as well as planning events into her week that she especially enjoys doing.

This chapter has explored the different dimensions that comprise the Toolbox and has illustrated how the provision of a more comprehensive range of interventions enables the practitioner to tackle the problem a learner faces from several different approaches. In the next chapter, the range of tools available will be considered as well as deciding which tools should be used to deal with which problem behaviour, through using the assessment questionnaire.

Further Reading

Friedberg, R. and McClure, J. (2002) *Clinical Practice of Cognitive Therapy with Children and Adolescents*. New York: Guilford Press.

Stallard, P. (2002) *Think Good – Feel Good*. Chichester: John Wiley and Sons.

The Assessment Questionnaire

For each dimension there are 10 indicative questions – indicative suggests looking for telltale signs that point us in a specific direction. The validity of the answers will depend on the knowledge the practitioner has of the young person who has the behavioural concern. Once all the dimensions are answered there will be a profile of the problem, broken down into the different parts. It is possible that the 10 questions may not fully reveal the relevance of any particular dimension to the problem that is under consideration, but to overcome this potential difficulty there is a summary question at the end of each dimension. This allows the practitioner, with personal knowledge of the learner and his/her circumstances, to rate out of 10 how relevant the specific dimension is in the overall assessment of the situation. This will mean that this score, when added to the number of YES answers given to the set of 10, could result in a maximum score out of 20 for each dimension. For example,

Number of YES responses = 10
Adult assessment = 8
Summary assessment score = 18

Those dimensions with the highest scores will indicate a definite need for tools to tackle those particular aspects of the problem. It is expected that any problem will require tools from different dimensions, because as stated previously, all problems are multifaceted and multifaceted problems need multifaceted solutions.

The Dimension Questions

Physiological – Indicative Assessment Questions

To help determine the degree of significance this dimension has to the problem being investigated, please answer the following questions, YES or NO.

1 Does the learner make frequent trips to the toilet?

2 Does the learner show facial colour changes – flushed or pale – on certain occasions?

3 Does the learner tremor with nervousness?

4 Does the learner seem hesitant and anxious?

5 Does the learner cry easily?

6 Does the learner complain of stomach and/or other body pains?

7 Does the learner seem to lack energy and motivation?

8 Is the learner less sociable than usual?

9 Does the learner sweat or show excessive discomfort when tests or challenges are presented?

10 Do their carers speak of bed-wetting or sleep disturbances, or changes in the child's usual routine?

Summary Question

On a scale of 1 to 10, how important do you think the physiological dimension is to a full understanding of the problem being investigated (1 of very little importance, 10 very important)?

Number of YES responses _____

Adult assessment _____

Summary assessment score _____

The Dimension Questions

Feelings – Indicative Assessment Questions

To help determine the degree of significance this dimension has to the problem being investigated, please answer the following questions YES or NO.

1   Has there been a change in the learner's eating habits recently?

2   Is the learner sleeping more than usual?

3   Does the learner talk of 'no one liking them'?

4   Is the learner unable to empathise with peers?

5   Does the learner seem to lack confidence in themselves?

6   Can the learner have difficulties in identifying their feelings appropriately?

7   Can the learner recognise feelings in others?

8   Has the learner lost interest in hobbies, activities?

9   Does the learner actively try to avoid existing friends?

10   Does the learner display mood swings?

Summary Question

On a scale of 1 to 10, how important do you think the feelings dimension is to a full understanding of the problem being investigated (1 of very little importance, 10 very important)?

Number of YES responses _____

Adult assessment _____

Summary assessment score _____

The Dimension Questions

Behavioural – Indicative Assessment Questions

To help determine the degree of significance this dimension has to the problem being investigated, please answer the following questions YES or NO.

1   Do there seem to be definite identifiable triggers to the learner's behaviour?

2   Are there predictable consequences to the learner's behaviour?

3   Can you identify rewards that the learner enjoys and seeks?

4   Is or has the learner been influenced by inappropriate role models?

5   Do sanctions and negative feedback make little difference to the problem behaviour?

6   Does the behaviour get worse when efforts are made to change it?

7   Is the problem behaviour more likely to occur with known adults and peers?

8   Does the problem behaviour avoid something unpleasant ?

9   Does the problem behaviour happen in specific contexts?

10   Do you think the problem behaviour is motivated to obtain something?

Summary Question

On a scale of 1 to 10, how important do you think the behavioural dimension is to a full understanding of the problem being investigated (1 of very little importance, 10 very important)?

Number of YES responses _____

Adult assessment _____

Summary assessment score _____

Photocopiable:

The Dimension Questions

Cognitive – Indicative Assessment Questions

To help determine the degree of significance this dimension has to the problem being investigated, please answer the following questions YES or NO.

1 Does the learner explain his/her failures in terms of a lack of ability?

2 Does the learner compare her/himself to peers, 'I'm not as clever as them'?

3 Is the learner unable to see the other person's point of view?

4 Does the learner believe that he/she is unpopular with peers, 'No one likes me'?

5 Does the learner display a negative attitude towards new challenges?

6 Is the learner unable to talk about his/her thoughts and feelings?

7 Does the learner make quick negative decisions about new challenges?

8 Does the learner show distorted thinking, 'I always make mistakes'?

9 Does the learner find it hard to picture her/himself being successful?

10 Does the learner rely heavily on adult or peer support in lesson and free time?

Summary Question

On a scale of 1 to 10, how important do you think the cognitive dimension is to a full understanding of the problem being investigated (1 of very little importance, 10 very important)?

Number of YES responses _____

Adult assessment _____

Summary assessment score _____

The Dimension Questions

Social – Indicative Assessment Questions

To help determine the degree of significance this dimension has to the problem being investigated, please answer the following questions YES or NO

1   Does the learner have difficulties interacting with peers?

2   Does the learner spend time with older or younger children?

3   Does the learner have more problem behaviour during playtimes?

4   Does the learner have a clear role in class, for example, clown, bully or victim?

5   Is the learner over-domineering with peers?

6   Is the learner unable to share and take turns?

7   Is the learner unable to make new friends confidently?

8   Does the learner have difficulties in obtaining help appropriately?

9   Would you describe the learner as being passive and withdrawn, a 'loner'?

10   Does the learner find it difficult to initiate and maintain conversations?

Summary Question

On a scale of 1 to 10, how important do you think the social dimension is to a full understanding of the problem being investigated (1 of very little importance, 10 very important)?

Number of YES responses _____

Adult assessment _____

Summary assessment score _____

Photocopiable:

Rob Long's Intervention Toolbox © Rob Long, 2009, SAGE Publications.

The Dimension Questions

Happiness – Indicative Assessment Questions

To help determine the degree of significance this dimension has to the problem being investigated, please answer the following questions YES or NO.

1   Does the learner have few close positive peer relationships?

2   Does the learner often complain of ill health?

3   Does the learner rarely exercise?

4   Does the learner find it difficult to readily recall happy memories?

5   Does the learner find adapting to normal changes, for example, new staff, difficult?

6   Does the learner seem to not enjoy and appreciate natural beauty, music and works of art?

7   Does the learner find it difficult to relax and play?

8   Is the learner unable to cope with setbacks and failures?

9   Does the learner have little awareness of his/her personal uniqueness, value and strengths?

10   Is the learner unable to sit and work persistently towards goals?

Summary Question

On a scale of 1 to 10, how important do you think the learners' happiness is to a full understanding of the problem being investigated (1 of very little importance, 10 very important)?

Number of YES responses _____

Adult assessment _____

Summary assessment score _____

Photocopiable:

Rob Long's Intervention Toolbox © Rob Long, 2009, SAGE Publications.

Summary of Scores

Physiological _____

Feelings _____

Behavioural _____

Cognitive _____

Social _____

Happiness _____

As a benchmark, any score above eight is a strong indication of the importance of this dimension to the problem being investigated. BUT an exception is made for the happiness dimension because of its importance, so if the score is four or above interventions will be considered.

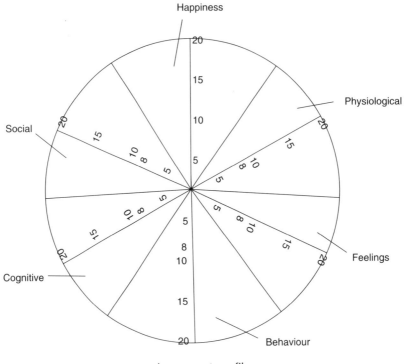

Assessment profile

Case Study 4.1   Kate, 9 years old

The Problem

Kate is 9 years old and is generally described by her teachers as being a 'bit of a loner'. Kate has few friends and acts in a passive way when faced with new situations, and will cry easily when not able to cope with new challenges. Her self-esteem is said by her parents to be 'rock bottom'. At home, Kate frequently talks about being left out of games and having no one to play with at school.

Her academic work is considered in the average range for her age. Though Kate rarely contributes in class, any homework is always completed to a good standard. Both school and home want to help Kate to be more confident and to enjoy school more.

The Assessment

This is completed by using the dimension questions as presented above, then totalling the number of YES answers for each section and adding in the score for the summary question. This will result in a profile of Kate's problem as follows:

Physiological 15

Feelings 17

Behaviour 4

Cognitive 16

Social 13

Happiness 6

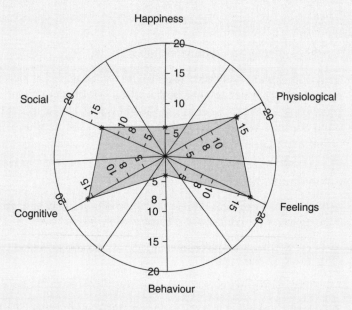

Figure 4.1   Kate's Assessment Profile

This profile of Kate enables the practitioner to then design a multifaceted intervention approach to her difficulties, concentrating mainly on the high-scoring

(Continued)

(Continued)

dimensions – namely, physiological, feelings, cognitive, social and happiness. If only one aspect were to be addressed then the chances of improvement would be greatly reduced. For example, it is of limited value for the practitioner to be working to raise Kate's self-esteem while her underlying belief that 'she is unlikeable' is not challenged and changed.

Interventions

Using Kate's personal profile enables the practitioner to choose from the MFI Toolbox those interventions that are most applicable. The following interventions are selected from a wider range of approaches which illustrate how they could be used to help in Kate's situation.

Physiological Dimension

Beneficial interventions would include:

Relaxation Skills: Any score above eight on this dimension can be seen as indicating the need for some of the relaxation tools being used. Kate's profile score was 15 and was especially significant in suggesting a low self-esteem.

Some relaxation tools are essential whenever there are indications of strong negative emotions, such as anxiety, nervousness, depression or anger. Such emotions will result in increased arousal within the learner's nervous system, which will be unpleasant and will also encourage negative thinking.

Feelings Dimension

Beneficial interventions would include:

Daily self-esteem activities: Tools to use will be aimed at increasing Kate's self-esteem. Which tools to specifically select will be dependent on the personal knowledge the practitioner has of the individual learner, but it is important that some activities are frequently undertaken with the goal of helping the learner to feel more positive about themselves.

Behavioural Dimension

As Kate has scored only four on this dimension, it is one area that does not indicate cause for concern and can be safely passed over.

Cognitive Dimension

Beneficial interventions would include cognitive restructuring activities, such as:

Balanced thinking: On Kate's scoring this dimension is clearly relevant. Kate has a range of negative thoughts about herself, which sadly are her attempt to understand why she is not included with her peers. Certain questions especially show her negative thoughts and these can become self-fulfilling if not challenged, possibly leading to a situation where Kate makes fewer and fewer efforts to change matters.

THE ASSESSMENT QUESTIONNAIRE 51

Social Dimension

Beneficial interventions would include:

Friendship Skills: Social tools need to be implemented that can help Kate improve how she approaches and relates to her peers. Specifically questions 1, 7 and 9 would indicate that this an important area which requires attention.

Happiness Dimension

Beneficial interventions would include:

Signature Strengths: Kate's Happiness score is borderline, and there could be a temptation not to include it, but a more complete approach would be to ensure that she is supported in enjoying herself in school and not being overwhelmed by the negativity occurring in her life.

The next chapter will provide detailed descriptions of the numerous tools available for each of the dimensions.

Example of an Intervention Log

○

| Tool Intervention Log for: Kate _____ |
| Designed by: Mr Long _____ Date: _____ |

Dimension	Tools	Date Used			
Physiological	Relaxation Skills				
Feelings	Daily Self-esteem Activities				
Behaviour	N/A				
Cognitive	Balanced Thinking				
Social	Friendship Skills				
Happiness	Signature Strengths				

A template for this intervention log can be found on the CD-Rom.

 Photocopiable:
Rob Long's Intervention Toolbox © Rob Long, 2009, SAGE Publications.

5

The Tools

hysiological

Physiological Tools

There are many tools available to help learners take control of their physiological arousal. Those listed below are some of the most effective but because all learners are unique individuals, it follows that what works for one might not necessarily work for another. As a practitioner it is your task to assist each learner to find the approach that works best.

When to Use Physiological Tools?

Some of the following interventions will be required when there is evidence of some physiological arousal associated with the problem behaviour, for example anxiety, anger and/or depression.

The Tools

Relaxation Training (RT)

It will come as no surprise that the antidote to being over-aroused is relaxation. Relaxation training (RT) is when there is a voluntary release of the tension an individual is experiencing. Relaxation changes the nerve impulses that are sent to the brain from the muscles. As a result, the individual feels calm psychologically as well as physically relaxed when a state of relaxation is achieved.

There are two essential components of RT. The child/young person needs to:

1 recognise the signs of physiological arousal and tension

2 have mastered specific relaxation techniques.

In order for a child or young person to learn to take control of their physiological responses they need to be able to recognise that they are becoming over-aroused, that is, they are tensing up.

Recognising Tension and Physiological Arousal Many children talk of feelings in certain parts of their body that can be identified as tension. For some it is a feeling of tightness in the face, or a physical clenching of the fists. For others, there is a

Physiological

feeling of pain in the stomach, a fast heart rate, a feeling of faintness or even sickness. Asking the child/young person the following questions can help enable a better recognition of tension:

• Where do you feel tension or discomfort?

• How does the tension or discomfort feel in your muscles?

• Do your muscles feel – stretched, hard, hurting or tired? Describe the feeling.

General Tension Scale   When working with children and young people it can help if they can describe the level of tension they feel by using a general measurement guide. The following 10-point scale can be frequently used to assess where their tension levels are before and after a relaxation exercise. It can also assist them in rating their level of arousal to different situations in school.

Tension Scale

Which situations make you feel tense? Circle the number which says most about how the following situations make you feel.

Thinking about school work:

very little				quite a bit					a lot
1	2	3	4	5	6	7	8	9	10

Being on my own:

very little				quite a bit					a lot
1	2	3	4	5	6	7	8	9	10

Being in class:

very little				quite a bit					a lot
1	2	3	4	5	6	7	8	9	10

Teachers:

very little				quite a bit					a lot
1	2	3	4	5	6	7	8	9	10

Support staff:

very little				quite a bit					a lot
1	2	3	4	5	6	7	8	9	10

Travelling to and from school:

very little				quite a bit					a lot
1	2	3	4	5	6	7	8	9	10

Being bored:

very little				quite a bit					a lot
1	2	3	4	5	6	7	8	9	10

Physiological

Once the assessment is complete the child/young person can then be helped to choose some Relaxation Techniques that will help reduce the level of stress experienced. The initial results of the assessment can be of value in the future because after a period of using these relaxation techniques the tension scale can be re-applied and any differences/improvements noted.

Relaxation Techniques
It may help with many of these exercises if the adult practises them personally prior to teaching a child or young person.

Progressive muscle relaxation   This involves beginning usually with the hands and gradually moving to different muscle groups in the body – calves, knees, thighs, bottom, etc. The muscles are tensed for 5–10 seconds then relaxed for 10 seconds. It is advisable to go for 75 per cent tension rather than fully strained. As each muscle group is tensed, encourage the child to breathe in and hold the breath and then to breathe out slowly with the relaxation, thinking 'relax' at the same time.

Not all of the muscle groups need to be worked on during a session. Several short sessions working on a few muscle groups are likely to be a more effective learning strategy in the long term.

At the end of the session the child sits quietly enjoying/experiencing the sensation of total body relaxation. Normal routines are then resumed in a calm manner. The more the relaxation sessions can become part of a daily or weekly routine the more effective they are likely to become. If they are done occasionally, they are less likely to be internalised by the child. Learning to relax can be easier for some than others. Encourage the child to practise whichever activities appeal to him/her throughout the day. The aim is for the child to not only use these relaxation techniques when he/she is tense but also to use them as part of a healthy daily routine.

Some guidelines to aim for:

• Establish a friendly relationship.

• Try for the same time each day/week.

• Remove distractions, noises, bright lights, etc.

• Use a calm, relaxed and quiet voice.

• Have the child/young person sitting in a relaxed posture.

• Ask them to breathe in deeply and exhale slowly while saying 'relax' to themselves.

• Repeat each exercise twice.

The core aim of progressive muscle relaxation is to systematically remove tension from different muscle groups in different body parts. What follows is an example script for achieving this, which is also included on the CD-Rom.

Practitioner to learner: 'We are going to help remove the tension you are feeling by concentrating on different parts of your body, starting with your hands. Make a fist with your hands and feel the tension in the muscles. Now open your hands slowly, releasing the tightness in all your fingers. Notice the change from tension to relaxation and how your muscles feel. Do the same again and feel the muscles in your hands becoming more and more relaxed'.

'Now progress to your arms. Bend your arms at the elbow and touch your shoulders, then allow them to return to a comfortable resting position by your sides. Notice the change of feeling from tension to relaxation. Do the same again and feel the muscles in your arms become more and more relaxed'.

The same process can then progress on to:

- Shoulders – pulling them up towards ears and then relaxing.

- Feet – screwing up toes tight and then releasing them.

- Stomach – taking a deep breath and holding it for three seconds while tightening stomach muscles and then breathing out slowly and evenly while relaxing.

- Face – clenching teeth together before releasing and letting the jaw rest with mouth closed and teeth slightly apart. Screwing the face up – nose wrinkled, eyes shut tight – before letting it all go and allowing the whole face to become smooth.

Allow the child to do each action twice to ensure that even more relaxation is achieved.

Finally, all over relaxation. Practitioner to learner: 'Now that you have worked through all of your muscles, check that you are relaxed all over.

Think of your hands and allow them to relax a little more,

think of your arms and allow them to relax a little more,

think of your hands and allow them to relax a little more,

think of your shoulders and allow them to relax a little more,

think of your feet and allow them to relax a little more,

think of your stomach and allow it to relax a little more,

think of your face and allow it to relax a little more'.

This exercise relies on the learner complying with the instructions. It is best to carry out such an exercise on individuals at first, some learners will find the concentration and the tasks easier to do than others and could be easily distracted if in the

Physiological

Physiological

company of peers. Remember, you are trying to help them find ways to control and release the tension that they experience when they feel angry or frustrated. It will be helpful having completed this exercise to refocus the learner prior to returning to the classroom. Talk with them about the tasks they will return to and equipment etc. that they will need, but, importantly, encourage them to practise some of this exercise throughout the day.

Breathing techniques

There are two types of breathing – chest breathing and abdominal breathing. Chest breathing is normal when an individual undertakes vigorous exercise and the body needs to replace oxygen, but this breathing is not appropriate for everyday activities. It is natural that when children feel frightened, afraid, confused, nervous, angry or upset that they hyperventilate. This fast over-breathing is intended to prepare the body for some form of reaction – fight or flight. However, this excessive breathing over and beyond what the body realistically needs can cause an unpleasant feeling and this can easily be misinterpreted, leading to an increase in the tension and arousal levels. Paradoxically, the sensation associated with over-breathing is of breathlessness – a shortage of air – leading to the child gasping or gulping in an attempt to obtain more air. This makes the whole situation worse and panic is more likely to occur.

Calm breathing technique   This is a simple breathing technique to return the person to a more natural abdominal breathing pattern. Ask the learner to breathe in through the nose to the count of seven slowly, then to breathe out through the mouth slowly to the count of 11. This is a quick way to increase slow and deep breathing.

Birthday candles   This tool is similar to calm breathing, but uses visualisation at the same time as encouraging slow and deep breathing. Ask the child to imagine there are 12 lighted birthday candles in a row. Ask the youngster to try to blow one out at a time each time they exhale. This exercise encourages the child to inhale and exhale in a normal relaxed way. The visualisation is useful especially in younger children as it encourages more effort and keeps them cognitively busy – an advantage for those who are prone to have worrying thoughts.

Visualisation

This task can be carried out with the whole class, the advantage being that the practitioner is quite clearly saying that these techniques are suitable for everyone. It could also be used as part of a movement or dance activity as a form of winding down at the end of the session. The following script is also available on the CD-Rom.

Ask the children to sit in a relaxed position with their eyes gently closed and to picture themselves on a sandy beach. Can they can feel the warm sun on their bodies? Ask them to create a picture in their minds as to where they are.

Leave a short time between each instruction, about 5 to 10 seconds, as you set the scene.

Can you hear any birds?

Can you smell the salty sea air?

Are you on your own?

Physiological

As the sun warms your body, you are becoming more and more relaxed.

As you look up in the sky, you see a small white cloud moving slowly.

As it moves across the sky, you feel more and more relaxed.

It is drifting away and you feel more and more relaxed.

As the sun warms your body, you feel more and more relaxed.

As the cloud drifts away, you feel more and more relaxed.

(Allow the children to stay in this relaxed state for some 20–30 seconds, then continue.)

When you are ready, open your eyes, you are ready to face the day in a relaxed and calm manner.

Activities described above can only be beneficial if they are practised on a regular basis. They do not take long and they are valuable skills for all learners, but some more than others.

Evocative Words

We experience the world through our language. So, through experiences and associations, words can come to evoke other thoughts and feelings. Words can act as triggers to encourage specific emotions, both negative and positive. If children have such thoughts as – 'I'm slow' or 'I'm stupid' – then these words will evoke negative emotions that support them.

By concentrating on more positive words children can be encouraged to feel more positively about themselves. Help the child or young person to choose the words that they most like and encourage them to practise repeating them in their head – as if they were a personal mantra. You could reinforce these by using the anchoring technique. That is, ask them what are the feelings they associate with this word. How do they feel inside? What thoughts do they have alongside this word? Now ask them to cross their fingers on one hand. Every time they cross their fingers this will remind them of their mantra and the positive feelings that they have with it.

Some examples of positive words:

strong   proud   determined   happy   trustworthy   dependable   kind   keen   funny   friendly   clever   Interested   honest   loveable   valued   belonging

Add others to the list which are appropriate for the age of the child.

Finger Pulse

Place the fingertips of each hand together. Close your eyes and change the pressure until you can feel the pulse in the fingertips at the contact point. Now breathe slowly and evenly and count your pulse rate. Count from 1 to 10 and when you reach 10 start again. (The actual pulse rate doesn't matter.) If you get distracted by thoughts, just start counting from 1 again. The important aim of this exercise is to

Physiological

keep concentrating on the pulse because as the child focuses on his/her body, the following changes will occur:

- ˙ The pulse will slow

- Hands will become warmer

- Body awareness will increase

- Any tension will reduce

- The child will become more relaxed.

A relaxed young person is not a stressed young person.

Remember, there are many other ways of helping children and young people to relax. The ideas suggested here may not be appropriate, but may prompt a different approach. The more comprehensive range of techniques you have available the better.

Conclusion

While all learners will benefit from learning about 'what's under the bonnet', so to speak, there will be some learners who are very prone to strong physiological responses in a range of situations. For this group the interventions detailed above will be extremely helpful in out-of-school situations as much as when they are in school.

Feelings Tools

Children with SEBD often stir up very negative feelings in the adults who teach and support them. These children are often:

- emotionally volatile

- frightened of failure

- slow to develop trust

- have poor academic and study skills.

'Children with SEBD can be the most difficult to teach and the hardest to like' (Bloomquist and Schnell, 2005).

Making sense of emotions is a serious challenge, yet it is emotions that are a significant part of the difficulties faced by many of these children. As a culture we often seek to protect children from negative emotions and assume that they cannot cope with painful events, using such euphemisms as 'Nanna has gone to sleep', for example, when a loved-one has died. However, in reality, children are much more likely to be harmed by untruths than truths. Some of the difficulties that many children have with feelings stem more from the many myths that they learn during early childhood. For example, myths such as, 'Big boys don't cry' or 'Time will heal'. Time in fact does not heal, we just become more able to cope with a situation. As a result, many children who face a wide range of challenges mask their true feelings. Boys can be more comfortable showing their anger rather than their sadness. Girls may feel forbidden to show their anger so may turn it in on themselves, and it may be expressed as self-harm. Whatever challenges children face, having a positive self-esteem is fundamental to them enjoying and succeeding in school.

When to Use Feelings Tools?

The problem behaviours that many learners face can result in them having negative relationships with key adults in their lives as well as poor peer relationships. Their work is also likely to suffer. There can, therefore, be many negative inputs with which the learner has to cope. As a result, it can often be expected for the learner's self-esteem to be low. Any score above eight on the feelings dimension is a clear indication of this and will justify a range of the following tools being utilised.

The Tools

Self-esteem Interventions

While all children are unique, there are interventions which will prove useful and relevant to them all. This is because of a very basic reason – they all have similar milestones to achieve in similar contexts. That is, the contexts of their family, their school work and their friendship groups.

Feelings

Boosting self-esteem Some tips and guidelines for developing self-esteem, as outlined by Hartas (2005), value a child's attempts and contribution – this may be through his/her work in the classroom, or through playtime activities. Enlisting the child to carry out classroom managerial roles, carrying messages, handing out or collecting in equipment and similar tasks, can give the practitioner the opportunity to show genuine appreciation for their help. Give children control through enabling them to make their own choices. If the practitioner can break a task down into its sub-tasks, the learner can be allowed to choose the order in which the work is done.

Developing a personal record of successes will allow a learner to more fully appreciate the progress they have made as an individual. By reviewing personal positive progress, a healthy, 'I will have a go' attitude can be encouraged. The record can include photographs of work as well as feedback from the practitioner, other staff and peers. A very simple example of a success log can be found on the accompanying CD-Rom.

Avoid making comparisons and competitions, this can demoralise many learners who will already have a tendency to compare themselves unfavourably with those more able than themselves. It is best if they are competing to beat their own past performances.

Teach and model emotional literacy skills, and then ask the learner how it feels when the new skill is mastered. Use yourself as a role model, talk out loud as you set a target, practise the necessary skills, and persist despite setbacks and frustrations.

Help the learner recognise and make positive self-statements about their personal qualities and competencies. When he/she has been successful in an area, help the learner understand the skills that have been employed and the personal qualities that were used and needed to succeed, for example, determination, creativity, planning, etc. before giving feedback.

Use books that contain characters that display empathy towards each other as well as qualities the practitioner would wish to develop in the learner. For example, primary-aged learners could read *The Little Engine that Could* by Watty Piper (2005). Secondary-aged learners could be asked to observe television personalities for their different attributes and qualities, and to discuss the circumstances that can make a quality positive or negative.

Building Relationships In every classroom, building relationships with learners is an essential skill but in achieving this the aim of the practitioner is to be friendly rather than become their friend. A good relationship depends on a commitment from both parties to establish a relationship and the opportunity to meet. Making time to have informal chats, before and after lessons, as well as in the breaktimes can allow for genuine interest to be shown. Noticing a new hairstyle or pair of trainers may seem trivial, but the event will be remembered by the learner. Similarly, making time to listen to children's views conveys interest in them as individuals and shows that they are valued for themselves and not a means to an end. A sure way to strengthen any relationship is to spend time with them as individuals. In school this can be achieved by joining in with extracurricular activities – a sure way of getting to know the child as a whole person.

Teaching Strategies   In the classroom, a learner's self-esteem can be strengthened when he/she receives specific praise, for example, 'I really like the way you have presented your plan in the introduction', or 'The colours you have chosen for your artwork show definite creativity', rather than a general 'Well done'. The tasks that the practitioner sets learners should be clear and meaningful for their goals. It is often helpful if learners are given the big picture and then the several steps are explained that will be taken to achieve it. When setting goals involve the learner as much as possible, agree a target to be worked towards and then develop an action plan, with small clearly defined steps, to ensure success. If a learner has some specific skill or knowledge – football skills, knowledge of animal welfare – involve them in showing or teaching others, a sure way to enhance status with peers and self, and a sense of personal value.

Personal Qualities   During one-to-one time, help the learner appreciate his/her own uniqueness by exploring likes and dislikes. What are their favourite meals, favourite television programmes and music, for example? The aim is to show that being different from others is not unusual in many areas of our lives. When learners are different from others because of the specific challenges they face, it is not uncommon for them to have negative feelings, shame and embarrassment. They see themselves as being different and so establishing their right to their uniqueness is very important. Producing a 'lifeline' of key events and key people in their lives can again reinforce the journey they have already taken and the many challenges they have faced and mastered.

Skill Development   Skills are learned best through receiving constructive feedback and lots of opportunities to practise them. Encouraging a learner to join clubs and other after-school activities to learn and develop new skills is a positive step. When starting new activities, setting up a 'buddy' system to offer support and someone to 'keep an eye out' can increase the likelihood of success. To reinforce skills once learnt, arrange for the learner to teach or support another pupil in the same area.

Frustration Control

Learners who lack the ability to self-regulate their feelings can find this leads to problems in a number of areas. Learning especially will be affected as these children are likely to become over-emotional when faced with work that challenges them. In addition, they may have friendship difficulties as their emotionally volatile nature may make them unpredictable – this can result in peers preferring to avoid them. Emotional self-regulation is clearly an important skill, one that is essential for young people if they are to achieve set goals, persevere and complete tasks and direct behaviour. The following are techniques to help learners manage frustration or at least manage it more effectively.

- Small steps – make sure that new tasks are broken down into smaller, more manageable ones.

- Reduce stimulation – if the learner becomes over-frustrated when playing with several peers, reduce the number of playmates to a more manageable number. It can also help if the game or activity is well structured, with specific rules to follow about how to play.

- Breaks – establish a routine with the child so that if he/she becomes frustrated a signal to staff will enable the adult to arrange for a break to be taken or a different activity to be started.

- Role models and stories – find television or sport heroes that persevere to overcome challenges. Use, or make up, stories about determination, for example, *The Little Engine that Could* (Piper, 2005).

- Pep talks – begin new tasks with a positive talk, review past challenges that have been mastered, for example, riding a bike, learning to swim, and emphasise the new skills that they are learning.

- Self-talk – help the learner to develop inner thoughts, that can help when facing new tasks – 'I know this will be hard for me, but I am going to keep trying, and if I get stuck, I will ask for help'.

- Relaxation skills – teach skills that can be used in moments of frustration to reduce the feelings of tension and anger. For example, counting back from 10 to 1, saying each number on the outward breath, focusing as much as possible on the breathing.

 - The Quick Relax Method – this needs to be practised and overlearnt to be of any use. This is also available to be printed off from the CD-Rom.

Step 1

Help the child recognise and become aware of those body signals that indicate that he/she is becoming tense and upset – such as sweaty palms, fast heart rate, rapid breathing, nervous tummy.

Step 2

Tell the child to smile inwardly, and say slowly, 'I can calm myself down'. This is a very important step, as it helps the child feel in control of the situation and not a victim of it – having skills to master the tension is a key step towards taking control.

Step 3

Tell the learner to imagine that his/her feet have small holes all over the surface. (This may seem a silly image but it is very effective.) Then ask the learner to imagine and try to feel cool air coming in through the holes and flowing up through their legs and into their stomach. Ask the child to hold the air in his/her stomach for the count of 12 down to 4, then to push the 'stressful air' down their body, back through their legs and out through the holes in their feet.

Step 4 (optional)

The learner can also be instructed to imagine going to a place where he/she feels fully relaxed and happy.

Explain to the learner that these steps can be carried out anywhere and that no one needs to be aware that these are being learned in order to control the stress and frustration that may be felt by the individual.

It is important that whatever skills are employed, the learner is encouraged to practise them frequently and on a regular basis. To be of value when a learner feels frustrated, the skills must have been fully mastered.

Anger Control

Anger is a normal emotional response to many situations – it involves the body being prepared for fight or flight. This means that when anger is felt as an emotion there is an increase in the hormones that are responsible for preparing a person for action. This response is controlled by old parts of the brain and is not dependent on thinking. As a person becomes aroused, the ability to think straight is reduced and this can result in a feeling of anger becoming transformed swiftly into action. Therefore, any efforts to help children manage their anger will involve three stages of strategy.

Stage 1: Identify What Makes You Feel Angry   The practitioner encourages the learner to list those situations that can result in feelings of anger and/or aggressive behaviour. Thoughts about different situations can be prompted with such questions and scenarios as:

- When do you feel angry?

- Do you get called names?

- Do people ask you lots of questions?

- Are you ever accused of something you didn't do?

- How do you feel if you can't do the work in class?

- Does anyone ever call you a liar?

- How do you feel when things you like get broken?

- Are you ever pushed in the playground?

- Are you told off for doing something that other pupils do – but they never seem to be punished?

- Do you forget to bring the correct equipment to school?

- How does it make you feel if a friend seems to prefer someone else to you?

- Are you told that a piece of work that you worked hard on is not good enough?

Stage 2: How do You Feel When You are Angry?   The learner needs to be aware that feeling angry in such situations is normal, but it is recognising when the strong feelings can prevent him/her from thinking sensibly about what to do. Recognising and listing the personal warning signals of anger is the next step.

When I am getting angry:

- My face goes red.

- I breathe faster than usual.

- I start to fidget.

- My voice sounds different.

- I feel tense in my stomach.

- My hands start to shake.

- My mouth feels dry.

Stage 3: What Could You do When You are Angry?   Once a learner understands the type of situation that triggers personal anger, and recognises the bodily responses that can occur, the more ability there will be to control the situation. Controlling the physical sensations of anger that can occur will require the essential use of some relaxation techniques. Reference to those techniques presented under physiological tools (pp. 53–60) or in frustration control (pp. 63–65) will be useful, namely – muscle relaxation and deep breathing techniques.

While different solutions to anger will suit different learners, here are some ideas to consider.

If the learner can recognise that he/she is becoming angry, there is the opportunity to teach avoidance tactics – walk away, sit somewhere different, engage in a different activity.

The practitioner could develop a verbal or visual cue understood solely by the learner, meaning, 'Stop what you are doing, and go and do another activity'. The activity would be one that had been previously agreed with the learner that allowed for a calming period, for example, colouring in or making a collage.

If the learner was too young to take full control of emotions, then the practitioner could develop a range of distraction techniques that would interest the learner, for example, 'Let's go and feed the hamster'.

Encourage learners to talk about their feelings. If they believe they have been treated unfairly – a common trigger for anger – listen and accept their points of view.

Learners should be fully aware of the consequences of their angry outbursts. While the aim should always be to distract and dissuade them from losing control, there need to be clearly agreed consequences to either hurting others, damaging property or disrupting lessons.

To actively involve the learner it might help to use such resources as *Don't Pop Your Cork on Mondays* by Moser (1988) – a simple story with practical ideas.

Alternatively, *Anger Management with Children* (Stringer and Mall, 1999) is a useful manual for practitioners with many practical activities to use.

Conclusion

The key feelings tools that have been detailed here are the most common ones that are associated with many problem behaviours. The reasons why so many learners need support are many and complex, but it is school staff who can enable all learners to acquire insight, understanding and skills to better enable them to cope with their emotional life.

Feelings

Behavioural

Behavioural Tools

The tools based on the behavioural approach focus on environmental factors. They each show how, in principle, a learner's behaviour can be changed by the way in which school staff respond to it. While originally based on laboratory studies, this approach has been found to be very effective in a wide range of social situations, including classrooms. The most powerful aspect of it is that if the circumstances are changed around a learner's behaviour, the behaviour itself can be changed. Most importantly, because practitioners have control over their own behaviour, by changing the way they respond to a learner, they can change the way a learner responds back – a powerful approach.

When to Use Behavioural Tools?

If the total score obtained for the behavioural dimension is over 10, that is from the set questions plus the summary question, then there is a definite need for tools from this dimension. The younger the learner the more likely it is that these tools will be needed because the emphasis with this approach is to change environmental factors, rather than expecting the learner to take control of their own behaviour.

The Tools

Each of the following behavioural tools will be referred to using a technical title as well as a more memorable user-friendly term, for example, 'low rates of responding', is better remembered as, 'little by little'.

Rewards or Positive Reinforcement (PR)

Positive Reinforcement is any consequence that increases the likelihood of a specific behaviour happening again. PR is something that the learner would like to have and any behaviour that is already occurring can be increased through the use of PR or rewards. There are different types of PR that are readily available within the classroom – non-verbal ones, such as a 'thumbs-up' or a smile, and verbal ones, from 'Well done', to 'That is awesome'. The more a PR is used the less effective it can become because of the process of habitualisation – the familiar loses its impact. Therefore, there is sometimes the need for practitioners to hold back on some PR in order to maintain its effectiveness. Tangible Positive Reinforcements are another option, including a wide choice from stickers to certificates. PRs offered as activities can include an extra five minutes on the computer, to choosing a special activity at the end of a lesson. Finally, there is the option of social PRs when learners' achievements and successes are recognised and awarded, for example, in a whole-school assembly, or when their work is displayed in the reception area. So from being told 'Well done' in class to receiving a certificate in front of the whole school or a free trip to a skating rink, there is a powerful set of Positive Reinforcements to use effectively. Care needs to be taken, however, that the reward has the desired effect. If a learner becomes embarrassed about being singled out for recognition and an award in front of his/her peers, or doesn't enjoy skating, the ultimate feeling may be one of punishment, not reward.

Little by Little – Reinforcement of Low Rates of Responding (RLR)

This involves staff in allowing for a number of agreed behaviours, but any more than the agreed amount would result in a sanction. For example, a child being out of his/her seat once or twice in a lesson might not constitute problem behaviour, but when it is 12 or more times and results in the disruption of others, then it can become a problem behaviour. The practitioner can use this intervention by agreeing with the learner an achievable reduction in problem behaviour, and a chosen reward (PR) for achieving the target.

Zero Tolerance – Reinforcement of Behaviour Omissions (RBO)

This technique is a rather extreme approach, where no behavioural infringements are allowed. It is similar to RLR, but instead of an agreed reduction in the problem behaviour, the reward is only obtained by the complete absence of the problem behaviour during an agreed time period. For learners with SEBD this approach is more likely to lead to a negative relationship with authority, as it is highly unlikely for them to be able to move directly from having the problem to eliminating it. It may be more appropriately used with very short time periods in mind, for example, 'If you do not shout out for the next five minutes, you will earn an extra five minutes on the computer'. Such an approach should aim to enable the learner to experience success, and then gradually increase the target time achieved.

'Catch 'em being good' – Reinforcement of Incompatible Behaviours (RIB)

Choose a behaviour that is incompatible with the problem behaviour, for example, the opposite of 'Being out of his seat' is 'Being in his seat'. The child is reinforced for doing the complete opposite to the behaviour that is seen as the problem. The aim is to always emphasise, reward and thereby increase the frequency in positive aspects of the child's behaviour that are incompatible with the identified problem behaviour.

Shaping

Choose a desired behaviour and break it down into small achievable steps. For example, the main goal could be 'Playing with peers without disputes.' This could be achieved through:

1   Reinforcing play alongside another child for a short time, perhaps 10 minutes.

2   Then reinforcing sharing with another child, for example, colouring when there is only one box of crayons so that sharing has to take place.

3   Finally, the learner might then be ready to play an interactive game with several peers, again for a fixed time of perhaps five minutes, resulting in a reward (PR) if this is successful.

Each of these above approaches utilises Positive Reinforcement in some form. The above activity is known as 'shaping' because it involves the building up of a number of behavioural skills from the simple to the more complex, but it also utilises Positive Reinforcement.

Self-monitoring, Self-evaluation and Self-reinforcement

These processes can be especially useful for those learners who are somewhat passive and disengaged from learning. At first, the learner needs to be assisted in learning

Behavioural

how to observe and objectively record his/her own behaviour – self-monitoring. The learner can then carry out a comparison of his/her performance to an agreed set standard – self-evaluation – before then giving themselves a reward if the agreed standard has been achieved – self-reinforcement.

 Case Study 5.1   Karl

Karl struggles to keep on task when doing individual maths work.

Karl is to monitor his correct responses on a maths worksheet and then compare his score to an agreed target.

If successful he can allow himself five minutes' free time on the computer.

 Case Study 5.2   Petra

Petra has a history of arriving at her morning class late and without the correct equipment.

Petra learns to monitor how many times during the week she arrives in class on time and with the correct equipment. Her score is compared to an agreed target.

 As a reward, she takes a special commendation home. (See the self-monitoring worksheet for class equipment and homework.)

 Case Study 5.3   Paul

Paul is frequently reprimanded for talking with others and not getting on with his own work.

Paul agrees to monitor his 'on-task behaviour'. Every time the teacher taps her table, he puts a tick or cross depending on whether or not he was on task (self-monitoring). At the end of a set period, the number of ticks are counted (self-evaluation).

 If an agreed score is achieved he can choose a game to play (self-reinforcement). (See the self-recording worksheet for paying attention.)

Functional Analysis of Behaviour (FAB)

This tool is a much more comprehensive way of tackling behavioural problems. A learner's behaviour can be seen as a way of coping in a particular situation. For example, if the work is too difficult and he/she becomes disruptive, the result can be the child's removal from the class, thereby resulting in a solution for the child, not a problem. Staff can often be drawn into focusing on the prevention of the inappropriate behaviour, and as a result often, unwittingly, help to maintain it. Functional Analysis of Behaviour emphasises teaching the learner alternative ways to behave when faced with difficult situations.

Behavioural

The Method: Stage 1 – Problem Clarification   Clearly define the problem behaviour (PB). Give a description of the PB in operational terms. That is, describe the behaviour in observable and measurable terms. The aim is for the description to be so clear that two independent observers would agree whether or not the problem behaviour had occurred.

For example, instead of saying Ronaldo is aggressive – a rather vague description – a more operational definition would be that Ronaldo hits other learners on the arm with enough force to hurt. Or, instead of describing Matt as often being disruptive, an operational definition would be that Matt calls out inappropriately, on average 18 times per lesson.

Stage 2 – Information Gathering   Collect information and data about the problem behaviour. This is very important in order to make sense of the problem behaviour and detect any patterns to it. The more detailed data that is collected, the clearer the picture will become and the more evident any patterns will become. A behavioural detective needs good information.

Working through set questions can be a useful way of collecting data.

- Where does the problem behaviour usually occur? Is it in a classroom, corridor or during free time?

- Does the problem behaviour occur more often in the morning or afternoon sessions?

- What activity or lesson was the child doing before the problem behaviour took place?

- Are you able to count how often the behaviour occurs? For example, the number of times the child is out of their seat, gets into a fight, or behaves defiantly?

This data will then be helpful when intervention tools are put into action, as any changes can be noted by comparing the frequency of the problem behaviour:

- Are the same people always present when the problem behaviour occurs?

- Does the behaviour take place more often with certain adults?

Consider the tasks or activities that are going on when the problem behaviour happens:

- Are there certain lessons, with certain types of work, written or oral tasks, being presented?

- Are the children working individually or as a group? If the behaviour is during playtime, what kind of activities are going on?

Finally, consider what kind of reactions result from the problem behaviour. How do any peers behave who are present? What are the responses of the adults who are present? What kind of sanctions does the learner receive because of the problem behaviour?

Behavioural

All of the above knowledge can be extremely useful when trying to change behaviour. Sometimes a small tactical change, such as moving where a learner sits in class, can bring about a vast improvement. Also, if the problem behaviour is a playtime issue, it may indicate that the learner lacks certain skills, such as how to join in and play effectively with others, and may, therefore, show where efforts should be made to make changes.

The data collected provides a rich picture of the contextual factors that are usually present for the problem behaviour to occur, in other words, the antecedents. These triggers are the cues that make the behaviour likely to occur. With the knowledge from the data collected, it is then possible to make some changes to the context to reduce the behaviour. If the behaviour occurs mostly when the learner is with specific individuals, then a reseating plan may be effective in solving the problem. Similarly, if the problem behaviour happens as a child's response to certain learning tasks, then providing additional support at this time may enable the learner to acquire the necessary skills with which to cope better.

Stage 3 – What is the Function of the Problem Behaviour?   This approach strongly believes that behaviour is functional, that there is a purpose to every behaviour and there is a need to consider why it takes place. The answer, more often than not, is contained in what the problem behaviour earns for the learner. The common functions of in-school problem behaviours are to obtain attention, to avoid work, to hurt others, to be nurtured or to be in charge. To ascertain the possible function of the behaviour for an individual there are key questions that can be asked.

Remember that often there will be more than one function to a behaviour – it may be motivated to both avoid work and gain attention from peers. Behaviour is complex and multidimensional – that is why there are probably many reasons why you are reading this book.

The questions below can assist in deciding which are the main functions behind a behaviour. Each set of questions is presented within the context of a case study, with some background information, an example of a specific event and followed by suggestions for a behavioural plan.

 Case Study 5.4   To Obtain Attention

Does the behaviour obtain more time or attention from either adults or peers? If the learner is asked to stop the problem behaviour, does he/she do so for a short while, but then start again? Does the behaviour tend to irritate and annoy you?

Background

Claire is a very popular and entertaining student in Year 9 who enjoys being the centre of attention, from staff and peers. In class, Claire needs frequent reminders to work at her own desk and complete set work. Her use of materials is often inappropriate – using books and rulers to drum. Unless fully engaged in her work, Claire enjoys being the class clown, and has a reputation for being dramatic. When requested to cease her behaviour, Claire will for a short time.

The Event

While being taught by a supply teacher, Claire's behaviour disrupts an entire lesson. Her attempts to mimic the class's favourite soap theme, while entertaining, leads to frequent reprimands and finally exclusion from the class.

Behaviour Plan Suggestions

- Give the child extra attention when she has behaved appropriately, and make sure she understands that this is the acceptable way to obtain attention.

- Reward periods of low problem behaviour and provide an agreed reward.

- Allow a set number of times to ask for support.

- Sit the child with a good role model.

- Involve the child in self-monitoring with an agreed target and reward.

- Give the child roles of responsibility that obtain attention from peers and adults.

- Ignore misbehaviour when possible, or delay any response to it. This shows the learner that the misbehaviour will not obtain the attention that she hopes to gain.

 ## Case Study 5.5   To Avoid Work

Does the learner have any learning difficulties? Is the work differentiated? Does the learner appear able to do the work, but is just not interested? Does the problem behaviour change depending on the kind of work set?

Background

Tim, 12 years old, is a very able learner who in specific lessons seems to switch off and daydream. He is not disruptive or defiant, but his teacher knows that he is underachieving. Discussions with home indicate no problems and when questioned, Tim just claims to be bored with the subject.

The Event

Tim's teacher organises some cooperative learning activities, where each student researches and records as part of their small team. Tim makes no effort to contribute and actively wanders away from his group to engage in different activities.

Behaviour Plan Suggestions

- Check the learner's ability and differentiate as appropriate.

- Is the work of interest to the learner, can the work be related to his interests?

(Continued)

Behavioural

(Continued)

- Negotiate with the learner the amount of work to be completed in a set time, with agreed rewards.

- Involve him in group work, with the learner carrying some responsibility for certain 'challenge questions and problems' that are within his capability – these can be gradually increased in difficulty.

- Use more interactive teaching methods, ask the class to write down their answers to questions and then get them to share these in partners.

- Check that there are no changes in family circumstances that would account for any change in behaviour.

- Discuss with colleagues whether the child's behaviour is the same in other areas.

 ## Case Study 5.6   To Hurt Others

Does the behaviour hurt or harm others? Has the learner experienced neglect or harm him/herself? Is the learner socially skilled in peer relationships? Does the problem behaviour make it difficult for people to like the learner? When asked to stop the problem behaviour does the learner sometimes reply to the effect, 'It's not fair, you are always picking on me?'

Background

Nick is in Year 9. His behaviour is becoming more and more concerning to staff. He will often behave in underhand and spiteful ways to other students. He has been seen scribbling across another student's work as well as pinching and pushing students smaller than himself. Nick is the eldest of three children, while a new baby is expected in a few months' time. When asked about his behaviour he always says that he is being picked on and that others do worse things than him. He believes his teachers 'have it in for him'.

The Event

Mike, a support assistant, observes Nick calling another student names during a lunchtime. When Mike asks Nick what the problem is, Nick just walks off, ignoring Mike completely. When Mike challenges him about his behaviour Nick is blatantly rude and says that he does not have to listen to Mike. Mike refers the situation to Nick's tutor who places Nick on detention.

Behaviour Plan Suggestions

- Teach the learner empathy skills by using emotional literacy materials. These would include learning to recognise emotions in themselves, combined with an understanding of how certain actions – being kind or being cruel for example – would typically result in certain emotions.

- Teach restorative problem-solving skills. This would involve the learner in being able to think through the consequences of his/her actions and how any damage caused to others has to be repaired through the actions chosen in order to make amends. The following questions are useful in using this approach – 'What have you done?', 'What was the consequence of your actions?', 'How can you make amends?' Also add, 'What can you learn from this for next time?'

- Raise learner's self-esteem (also see pp. 61–65). Enable the learner to help others in areas where he/she has some competency.

- Ensure adult supervision at times when the problem behaviour is most likely to occur.

 ## Case Study 5.7   To be Nurtured

Does the behaviour lead to care and sympathy from others? Does the problem behaviour cease when one-to-one attention is given? Does the learner sometimes become the class victim or mascot? If asked to stop the behaviour, does the learner say, in effect, he/she can't cope?

Background

Sam is a lonely child in Year 3. He rarely mixes spontaneously with his peers and is often reluctant to leave class at breaks. In class, his work output is variable. He responds well when supported by a support assistant – Jane. Staff are concerned that he is becoming overdependent on her and will not make much of an attempt at any work until she sits with him. When she is working with other children he will leave his seat and pester her for help. When Jane is supervising lunch he will firmly attach himself to her and follow her around.

The Event

The event that concerns Jane happens just before the morning playtime. Sam is given a set task to work on as part of a group. Sam not only refuses to join in with the group, but runs out of the class and is found, by Jane, in one of the cloakrooms. He does not seem to have an explanation for his behaviour but says that he hates coming to school. Jane takes him back to his class, but feels that nothing is changing for Sam and that his behaviour is likely to go from bad to worse.

Behaviour Plan Suggestions

- Find out the learner's interests and use this information when you talk with him but also in class work.

- Support the learner in learning skills that can help him mix with his peers and help develop a circle of friends for him. This involves a technique where a group of children are willing to volunteer to support a peer with friendship difficulties. (For further information a useful link is www.inclusive-solutions.com.)

(Continued)

(Continued)

- Provide somewhere quiet and safe where he can go during breaks.

- Make yourself available for one-to-one, personalised time, to review his progress.

- Buddy him up with a supportive role model.

- Help him to set goals for the skills he is working to develop or improve.

 Case Study 5.8   To be in Charge

Does the behaviour lead to confrontations? If asked to stop the behaviour, does the problem behaviour happen again or get worse? Does the problem behaviour make you feel angry and/or exasperated?

Background

Charlotte is an extremely defiant Year 6 student who has recently joined her new school. Her behaviour can be very bossy towards her peers and at times she will use inappropriate language towards school staff. In class, Charlotte will refuse reasonable requests to help, and is especially defiant to the support staff. Her peers find it difficult to include her in their activities as she can be overpowering.

The Event

Charlotte is asked by the teaching assistant to help three other pupils to organise books and equipment. Charlotte blatantly refuses and makes it plain in rude language that the assistant can't make her do anything.

Behaviour Plan Suggestions

- The individual learner could be given the responsibility of teaching a skill he/she has mastered to another group of pupils.

- Involve the learner in developing guidelines for her appropriate classroom behaviour.

- Collect ideas from the learner about the kind of rewards she would like. Rewards that are motivating need to have some meaning or relevance to them.

- Support her in displaying her work to others.

- Encourage her to take up positions of responsibility. For example, on the school student council or in a classroom management role – being in charge of equipment and handing out resources.

- Set a choice of tasks, one of which she is to complete within a set time.

- Agree a 'Bin the Sin' system to make amends for any hurt caused by her behaviour. For example, if she has hurt or upset a peer she might have to use her breaktime employed in an activity to cheer the individual up, or if she spoils a piece of work she has to reproduce the spoilt material. (This technique is not dissimilar to Restorative Justice.) This encourages the learner to become aware of the consequences of her behaviour.

Stage 4   Monitor and evaluate effectiveness of the behaviour intervention plan.

Stage 5   Modify behaviour plan, if needed.

Conclusion

The behavioural tools are very effective as they rely on the adults involved in the situation changing some aspect of the behavioural context. This change then results in a change in the learner's behaviour. Through an understanding of how the problem behaviour relates to any specific context, interventions can be easily implemented and, through a persistent approach, can produce changes. There needs to be a degree of persistence as there is often a reluctance on behalf of the learner to change those behaviours with which they are familiar and which obtain goals for them.

Behavioural

Cognitive Tools

In the early formative years, children learn to make sense of themselves and their world. Language gradually enables them to remember yesterday and plan for tomorrow, while repeated experiences are internalised and used to predict future outcomes.

A child's internal logic could sound like this:

> If I receive love and appropriate attention whenever I am distressed, then I am highly likely to see the adults who care for me as being trustworthy. This internalised belief will lead me to expect care from all new adults I meet. If, however, my carers are not responsive and caring about my needs I am more likely to learn to distrust and fear adults. This thought can generalise to other adults, making me a suspicious and difficult child to reach.

Practitioners often meet hostile children who seem to use attack as their best form of defence. They seem to have a belief that the world is a hostile place, and that the best form of defence is offence. This is supported by research carried out by Dodge, Bates and Pettit (1990) in which cartoon clips of unpleasant events were shown to 300 five-year-olds – some of the children within the group had experienced abuse and neglect. They found that those children who had suffered abuse were:

- less aware of social cues

- more likely to see hostile intentions

- less able to give solutions to problems posed.

The conclusion drawn from this research was that the experience of being abused led children to see the world as a hostile, threatening place. For example, if such a child was pushed in the playground the response was more likely to be that they pushed back. There was evidence of a negative subconscious way of interpreting events in the light of past experiences.

The emphasis on learners having a good self-esteem has not been misguided, but it fails to tackle a more fundamental issue, the learners' core beliefs about themselves and learning – for success a learner needs to be more than just confident. From an early age core beliefs are developed that become so familiar to the individual that they can pass seemingly unnoticed. These beliefs are ways in which sense is made of how the individual relates to the world. These 'words in your heart' (Seligman, 1996) determine how a person responds to situations. 'It is not things themselves that disturb us but the view we take of them' (Epitectus).

In many classrooms there are children who, for numerous reasons, have a negative attitude towards learning, towards the adults who support them and their peers. Key techniques are now discussed to challenge the distorted core beliefs that hold many learners back from achieving their potential or relating positively to adults or peers.

When to use Cognitive Tools?

These tools will be important for all problem behaviours, but they will be of special value for those children who face such difficulties as speech and communication problems, learning difficulties, dyslexia, dyscalculia and dispraxia. Also, children who are either in foster homes or 'looked after' are also highly vulnerable to negative self-belief. It is worth detailing here two related processes that underpin the tools that will follow.

Cognitive restructuring refers to general efforts to change a way a child thinks, moving from being rather pessimistic towards more optimistic. Attribution retraining is a more specific technique to change the way a child explains the reasons for behaviours. For example, 'I succeeded because I studied hard', instead of 'I succeeded because I was lucky', or 'the questions were easy'. The first comment reflects internal control as an explanation while the latter show external control – factors outside the person determining the outcome.

If the total score obtained from the cognitive dimension of the questionnaire is over eight, then there is a definite need for tools from this dimension.

The tools

Linking Thoughts, Feelings and Actions
The more the learner understands the link between thoughts, feelings and actions, then the more likely the techniques are to work.

What we think affects our actions – 'I think you like me so I smile when we meet'.

What we think affects how we feel – 'I think you like me so I enjoy being with you'.

What we do affects what we think – 'I avoid the playground because I think I might get hurt'.

Depending on the cognitive ability of the child use one of the following two exercises to help establish the links.

Exercise 1: Thoughts and Feelings   This exercise is most appropriate for primary-aged children, but can be adapted for secondary. It will take approximately 20 minutes and its effectiveness can be seen when the learner can see the link between thoughts, feelings and actions in other everyday situations.

The story lends itself to a simple cartoon character. It can be changed to include the latest mobile phone or computer game in use instead of a kite (Friedberg and McClure, 2002).

Part 1   Once there was a little boy/girl (use the same gender as the learner and ask the child to think up a name for this character, for example Sam). Now, Sam really loved kites and he had seen a bright red and yellow one in a shop near where he lived. Sam thought that if he had a kite like that he would be the happiest boy in the world. Then, on his birthday he was given the kite by his family.

Ask the learner – How do you think Sam felt? And what do you think Sam was thinking?

Key Points

- Involve the child as much as possible in all parts of the story. Break down the thinking, feeling and action parts of the story into simple and specific terms.

- Summarise the story and check for understanding.

Part 2   Do you know what happened next? A really strong gust of wind pulled the kite out of Sam's hand and it went flying far away.

Ask the learner – Do you think Sam will still be happy? Can you draw a face of how Sam is feeling? What do you think Sam will be thinking now? What has changed?

Discuss the situation in simple terms with the learner – Sam felt good and had happy thoughts when he had a kite, but when he lost it all that changed. Help the learner make the link between what we think and feel and what happens to us. The effectiveness of this exercise can be seen when the learner can identify the link between thoughts, feelings and actions in other everyday situations.

Exercise 2: Three-Step Push Button Emotional Change Technique   This exercise is most appropriate for secondary-aged children. It will take approximately 20 minutes and its effectiveness can be seen when the learner can use the technique to control and change his/her negative feelings. The approach was devised by Alfred Adler (1969) and aims to teach how thoughts can change feelings.

Preparation and Validation   Firstly, talk about negative feelings and that it is OK for the individual with those type of feelings to feel bad and annoyed when people say 'Cheer up' or 'Snap out of it'. Sometimes if the learner is in a bad mood it is all right to just accept it and feel bad. BUT if the individual wants to change the mood then it is possible.

Step 1: Firstly, enable the learner to recognise the negative feeling for what it is:

- sadness

- anger

- depression.

Then, explore together how these different moods can be safely expressed, for example, by punching a pillow, painting, drawing, shouting, crying, grimacing, fist-shaking, kicking a ball, writing a letter.

Step 2: Thinking can be described as the button that can be pushed to change a bad feeling into a good one. Enable the young person to explore what makes him/her laugh, or what is funny. It could be something that the adult may not find particularly funny at all!

Allow the learner to practise thinking about these thoughts, and for him/her to be aware of a change of mood, a lifting of spirits, that occurs. Discuss with the learner how to think of this humorous situation the next time he/she feels sad or depressed so that a new, more positive feeling is allowed to replace the negative one.

The individual now has a quick technique that can be practised to change his/her state of feeling, anytime and anywhere. If the learner is readily able to do this, then explore those thoughts that can also lead to feelings of anger and sadness.

Step 3: If appropriate, explain the 'contagion principle'. This can be described as the tendency to 'catch' feelings from other people. If children are in a good mood they are likely to influence other friends into a good mood as well. Check if the young person knows how to get Mum or Dad into a good mood and if this technique also works on specific teachers. This is furthering the young person's knowledge about feelings and how he/she can have a strong degree of control over not only personal feelings but other people's feelings as well.

Thought Identification and Balanced Thinking

The following two exercises are useful for upper-primary and secondary-aged learners, taking approximately 30 minutes. The effectiveness can be observed when the learner can use the technique to control and change negative feelings.

There are numerous activities that can be used to help learners think more clearly and manage negative thoughts but many of them need to be used in conjunction with each other. For example, thought identification will need to be followed by balanced thinking. The learner needs to have identified specific thoughts before challenging them.

Thought Identification   Help the learner to identify the negative thoughts that pop into his/her head when faced with certain situations and challenges – personal awareness is an important first step. Enable the learner to identify the specifics about the event because more detail gives a clearer picture of the scenario. For example, Was the child in the playground or classroom? Did the negative thoughts occur when there was a certain type of work to do? When the negative thoughts occurred, were you with anyone? Allow the child to describe the situation in detail, and what thoughts and feelings were occurring. Refer back to the previous story to reinforce the link between thoughts and feelings.

Balanced Thinking   After identifying negative thoughts linked to a specific event, for example, 'I'm going to get this wrong because I'm no good at writing', work through the following questions with the learner:

- Is there hard evidence to support this thought?

- What would your best friend say to you, if he/she heard you thinking in this way?

- What would you say to your best friend if he/she had this thought?

Balanced thinking is not trying to deny reality, but give a balanced view, rather than an all-or-nothing approach. Balanced thinking is about helping the learner to

Cognitive

Cognitive

include more information, to ask useful questions, to not accept negative thoughts as being totally correct – negative thinking tries to ignore positive information.

Thought Stopping

This exercise is most appropriate for secondary-level pupils. It will take approximately 10 minutes and its effectiveness can be observed when the learner can use the technique to report control over negative thoughts that interfere with success.

Thoughts are like water that makes a pathway in the sand because of the track that it always follows. The more we think about situations in a certain way, then the more likely it is that the same thought pattern will occur the next time we are in a similar situation.

Wearing an elastic band around the wrist can help a pupil break negative thought habits. By snapping the band against his/her wrist whenever a negative thought occurs, this helps to stop the train of thought, and to remind him/her that it is a thought that can be controlled.

Another simple idea is to take a negative thought and associate it with a tune that makes the pupil smile/laugh. Then, whenever the thought occurs, there is a tendency to hear the tune coming along with it. It takes practice, but then breaking any over-learned habits will always take some effort!

Another technique is to record all of the negative thoughts that have occurred by the end of the day – write them down on paper or type them out and print them on a computer. Then, screw up or tear up the paper and throw those useless thoughts into the rubbish bin, where they belong.

Giving the pupil strategies to deal with the negative thoughts is the first step towards taking control and mastering them. Allowing the learner to give up is the easy but unhelpful option.

Remember, helping a learner to control his/her thinking is not a quick-fix option, it takes time. The individual will need to explore a number of methods to find which works for him/her personally. Some techniques will not work, but the more practice is achieved the more effective any technique is likely to become.

Take Command

This exercise is most appropriate for upper-primary and secondary learners. It will take approximately 20 minutes and its effectiveness can be observed when the pupil can clearly and readily make the distinction between the different types of statements.

This activity involves the learner reading a set of statements and deciding whether each statement shows self-control, or self-blame. The aim is for the child to understand that many thoughts just do not help towards gaining control. It is only through recognising these thoughts that they can be challenged and changed.

Draw a line with self-control at one end, and self-blame at the other. Check that the learner understands the difference between thoughts that are self-blaming and those that are about self-control to improve matters. If certain persistent and negative self-blame thoughts are identified, then they can be used in the previous balanced thinking exercise.

With the learner, discuss the following statements and ask him/her to choose which ones most closely describe their situation. The aim is to support and encourage the statements that reflect personal responsibility. The learner puts a mark on the line to show where they think each statement belongs. A worksheet for the learner can be found on the CD-Rom.

Self-control   *Self-blame*

I'm stupid, the others are cleverer than me.
I messed up on that test, I'll need to practise more.

Self-control   *Self-blame*

I get called names because no one likes me.
I will join a lunchtime club and meet new people.

Self-control   *Self-blame*

I can never remember what I'm told.
I will get a notebook to write down tasks to do.

Self-control   *Self-blame*

I failed the spelling test.
I will make cards and read them over.

Self-control   *Self-blame*

I get distracted where I sit.
I will ask to be moved.

Task Engagement

This exercise is appropriate for primary and secondary learners. It will take approximately 20 minutes and its effectiveness can be observed when the pupil can approach new tasks, using the different steps.

The following is adapted from a model by Croll and Hastings (1996) and can be used to help learners explore specific tasks in a way that will develop constructive and positive thinking. A worksheet for the learner to refer to as you go through this process can be found on the CD-Rom.

Firstly, with the learner find a task that is to be completed.

Step 1: Set the Task

_____

_____

_____

_____

Step 2: Action Plan   The following questions will help the learner systematically analyse the nuts and bolts of the task as well as his/her attitude and feelings towards it.

Key Questions

1   What needs to be done to complete the task?

2   What will be the completed goal?

3   What resources are needed to complete the task?

4   What skills and qualities are needed?

5   How long will the task take to complete?

6   How difficult is the task? Indicate this on a scale of 1 to 10, where 1 is not very difficult, 10 is very difficult.

7   How interesting is the task? Indicate this on a scale of 1 to 10, where 1 is not very interesting, 10 is very interesting.

Add further questions if appropriate:

8   _____

9   _____

10 _____

This discussion should last no longer than five minutes and should include ideas to overcome any identified difficulties.

Step 3: Task Review   At this stage draw the learner's attention to the progress made and how this was achieved. This increases a student's sense of competency and shows that success depends on effort, not only ability and luck.

Key Questions

1   To what extent were the goals achieved?

2   Was the plan a good one?

3   What improvements could be made?

4   Was it as difficult as expected?

5   Was it as interesting as expected?

6   _____

7   _____

8 _____

9 _____

10 _____

New Goals   With the learner explore the next goals that need to be set and encourage the learner to work through the same steps again.

Attribution Retraining

This exercise is most appropriate for secondary learners and will take approximately 20 minutes. Its effectiveness can be observed when the learner can clearly and readily make the distinction between the different types of statements.

When pupils use strategies that are ultimately self-defeating – such as withholding effort, cheating, procrastination – their goal is actually to protect their sense of self-worth. Attribution retraining involves modelling – that is, the learner hearing and seeing the steps an adult takes to tackle a problem. For example, 'I will need to break this task down into smaller parts if I am going to make progress'. The most important part of attribution retraining is providing many opportunities for the learner to practise.

The goals are to help learners:

1   concentrate on the tasks rather than becoming distracted by fear of failure

2   respond to frustration by retracing their steps to find mistakes or working out alternative ways of approaching a problem instead of giving up

3   attribute their failures to insufficient effort, lack of information, or reliance on ineffective strategies rather than to lack of ability.

When undertaking attribution retraining help the learner see that the effort involved in learning a new task is an investment towards success, rather than a risk that involves failure. The learner cannot hope to succeed without effort. As progress is made, show the child and emphasise how skills are increasing in a specific area. A key task for the practitioner as the child's supporter is to focus on how well new skills are being mastered, through the child's own effort and perseverance.

The potential pay-off to this approach is having students who value learning for its own sake. This is priceless and so it is crucial for school and home to devote themselves fully to encouraging, maintaining, and rekindling pupils' motivation to learn.

Restorative Problem Solving

This exercise is most appropriate for upper-primary and secondary learners. It will take approximately 10 minutes and its effectiveness can be seen when the learner understands the consequences of the behaviour on other people. It is a very good example of how to turn behavioural mistakes into learning opportunities.

Cognitive

Cognitive

Question 1: What Happened?   Instead of focusing on 'why' a behavioural problem occurred – the reasons are usually complex and not fully understood by the individual – it is better to ask, What happened? With sensitive questioning this should produce a clearer account of what took place. The fact that no blame is attributed can help the perpetrator give a more honest account of his behaviour. For example, 'I pushed Tim in the playground and he fell over'.

Question 2: Who has Been Affected and How?   The next line of questioning is aimed at helping the learner understand the consequences of his actions. To continue the example of Tim being pushed, the consequences might be that he fell over and started crying. Again, reasons for the actions are not the focus. Through staying with the actual event, the learner is being asked to focus on the actions and the consequences in a non-judgemental manner. It can be expected that children will make behavioural mistakes as they do not yet have an adult repertoire for coping in difficult situations, but future behaviour can depend upon how these mistakes are handled at the time.

Question 3: How Can the Situation Make Things Better?   This is the restorative phase of the exercise. How can the perpetrator make amends? Saying 'sorry' can be far too easy and no real learning from the incident will have been achieved. If someone has been hurt then the perpetrator could make amends through some activity to cheer up the victim, for example, by drawing a picture or by being their special buddy for the day. If the problem has been the disrupting of a lesson, then giving up time to make something constructive for the classroom might again be a better consequence than being kept in at breaktime.

Question 4: What Have we Learnt to Help us Make Better Choices Next Time? This is when alternative behaviours could be explored that could prove useful in the future. The learner could be given some specific tasks to practise in order to help them cope better next time.

Personal Responsibility and Self-understanding
This exercise is most appropriate for secondary learners and will take approximately 10 minutes. Its effectiveness can be seen when the learner understands that when poor behavioural choices are made, there is an expectation that he/she will analyse the choices, understand them and learn from them. A worksheet can be found on the CD-Rom.

A simple log sheet can be used to systematically work through a problem behaviour. Working with the learner, the incident is dated and recorded, in as much detail as possible. Questions asking 'who', 'what', 'where', 'when' can be used – 'Who were you with?', 'What were you doing?', 'Where were you and when did it happen?'

Next, and more difficult, is questioning how the individual contributed to the problem. Is the learner able to see and take responsibility for specific actions that led to the problem occurring? If so, can he/she consider alternative actions that would have prevented the problem? This can lead into thinking about and possibly practising alternatives. Sometimes this approach will not seem to work initially and it can be much to expect from learners to stand back and reflect on their actions.

Cognitive

However, just because it does not work at first should not discourage practitioners from introducing elements of it. Gradually breakthroughs can take place and insight and personal responsibility achieved by learners.

Example Log Sheet

Date of incident _____

What happened, where did it happen, who was involved? _____

I feel I contributed to the incident because _____

I think that _____ contributed when s/he _____

It would not have happened if I had _____

When I think back on what happened, I wish _____

Next time something like this happens, I will _____

Challenging the Negative De-catastrophising

This exercise is most appropriate for secondary learners and it will take approximately 20 minutes. Its effectiveness can be observed when the learner can talk through difficult situations, seeing positively how he/she can learn to cope with them. A worksheet for the learner can be found on the CD-Rom. Often, learners can 'awfulise' a situation. That is, the learner imagines the worst consequences possible – a trait that can persist into adult life. The individual looks at the world through a negative framework and can only see the worst outcomes – the glass is always half empty, never half full.

This exercise involves the adult choosing situations that the learner does not like and helping the learner imagine the worst outcomes that could possibly happen in those situations. The adult's role is to bring a sense of perspective to the situation. Learners will often imagine consequences that are highly unlikely, unrealistic and even impossible. The type of difficult scenarios selected should be school based.

The practitioner helps the pupil choose a learning situation he/she does not like.

_____

_____

Explore with the learner the realistic consequences:

What is the worst thing that could happen to you in this situation?

_____

_____

_____

And the best outcomes:

Cognitive

What would be the best thing that could happen to you?

_____

_____

_____

Try to bring out in reality what is the most likely outcome.

What do you think is most likely to happen?

_____

_____

_____

The resulting ways of coping with the situation may well lead into specific skills that the learner needs to either acquire or perform well.

If the worst thing happened – what could you do to cope?

_____

_____

_____

Positive Thinking

This exercise is appropriate for all learners and it will take approximately 20 minutes. Its effectiveness is observed through learners being able to recall positive school-based memories, instead of negative ones.

There is a tendency for many learners to have an automatic negative framework that results in them always noticing failures, conflicts and/or unhappy times. This exercise helps them to think positively and reframe situations, so that 'I can't' becomes 'I will try', and 'I'm going to fail' becomes 'I will have a try'.

The practitioner enables the learner to complete the sentences presented below. If a sentence is too difficult for the learner then the practitioner quickly moves on to the next, trying to create a mental set of thinking positively. On completion, the practitioner can add any areas that are especially relevant for the individual pupil. The learner then chooses two or three sentences to remember and repeat to the adult on request. A worksheet for the learner can be found on the CD-Rom.

Make a list of positive things about yourself.

1   One thing I like about myself in school is _____

2   In school I look forward to _____

Cognitive

3 When I am at school I feel good about _____

4 A favourite school memory I have is _____

5 Something I do well in school is _____

6 A recent success I had in school was when I _____

7 I know I can _____

8 I am at my best when I _____

9 One of my best qualities is _____

10 Friends can rely on me to _____

11 My favourite school trip was _____

12 If I had to say one good thing about me, it is _____

13 A recent problem I solved was _____

14 A skill I have mastered is _____

15 People in school like it when I _____

Add more and help the learner choose two or three to practise each day.

Conclusion

Changing the core beliefs that a learner has is not an easy task and there is no quick-fix solution. The choice of techniques used to improve a learner's self-belief will be dependent upon the individual's cognitive level of understanding. Developing a positive thinking style in a learner will be essential to enable him/her to cope with and hopefully overcome any problem behaviours.

Social

Social Tools

It appears that today, schools are becoming more involved in the role of socialising many children and young people into the values of caring, sharing and helping – skills that would have originally been taught and learnt at home. This preschool social education cannot be assumed nowadays and the tools in this section are aimed at helping those learners who find it difficult to work cooperatively in class or relate positively with their peers during free time.

When to use Social Tools?

Learners will benefit from these skills if they are experiencing difficulties with their peers, often highlighted by the number of problems they have during free time. Most young people learn intuitively such key skills as how to make friends and how to be a friend, but for those who find this a problem, for whatever reason, then focused support is essential.

The Tools

Performance Skills
It is useful to ask a key question when considering problems with social skills – is the difficulty performance-related or is there a skill deficit?

Performance-related means that the child has the social skills that are required but does not choose to perform them. For example, the pupil is polite and respectful to teachers but rude and offensive to support staff – 'You're not a teacher' attitude.

You may find it helpful to answer the following performance-related assessment, which is available to print from the CD-Rom.

 Does the learner:

1   Perform the skills in some situations but not others? YES/NO

2   Have adults who like him, and those who don't? YES/NO

3   Perform the skills if rewarded? YES/NO

4   Show the skills under threat of sanctions? YES/NO

5   Change behaviour according to the status of the adult? YES/NO

6   Behave differently according to the gender of the adult? YES/NO

7   Seem popular with peers? YES/NO

8   Have good days and bad ones? YES/NO

9   Seem motivated to hurt adults or peers? YES/NO

10 Show insight into how the behaviour affects others? YES/NO

If there is a score of five or more YES answers then there is a clearer indication that the problem is performance-related.

Respect

The one common performance-related concern that is usually expressed is that of respect – or lack of it. Many adults in schools today feel that a key problem is the lack of respect that they receive from learners – this is true for primary staff as well as secondary staff. This problem is highlighted by the fact that while many of these children and young people have the necessary skills to be respectful they choose not to use them.

The *Oxford Dictionary* (1956) defines the verb 'respect' as:

> To avoid degrading or insulting or injuring or interfering with or interrupting, treat with consideration, refrain from unworthy conduct or thoughts.

Such a definition would meet with the approval of most school staff.

It is an extremely complex area to explore why some children/young people are disrespectful towards adults in school. There are many different explanations and instances, but it is important here to try to analyse and understand the behaviour rather than personalise it. Typically, this type of behaviour is repeated by a few individuals and so there are likely to be some common undercurrents that can be considered in an attempt to explain such behaviours.

In the classroom it may be guilt through association. This explanation would fit those instances where the learner is being presented with work that they either can't or believe they can't do. The person/s who are in control of setting this work can be caught up in their frustration maelstrom, resulting in a 'shoot the messenger' syndrome.

Disrespect in the playground may be caused through rebelliousness. When the learners are in the classroom they are controlled, their movements and all general freedoms under the direction of one or two adults – one usually being a teacher with power and status. The classroom is an artificial context where the learner is usually treated as part of a group rather than a person. He finds himself in close proximity to other learners with whom he may not normally mix, but there is no choice and he is told where to sit or when to talk, etc. Free time is a period in stark contrast, where pupils can go and do as they please, mix with whoever they choose. So when adults seek to control the pupils' behaviours in this context it appears that the adults are encroaching on precious personal time. The behavioural responses of disrespect can be linked to a young person's demand for personal autonomy. This can be combined with the perceived lower status and power of the playtime staff compared to the teachers in the classroom – seeming to give permission for rudeness and disrespectful behaviour.

It is known that learners who are disrespectful do not treat other people as they would wish to be treated themselves and are not considerate towards other people's feelings. They often have difficulties accepting people who are different from themselves, fail to resolve any differences of opinion in a polite way and can frequently tease or ridicule people.

Social

 Case Study 5.9   Project Respect

A small rural primary school was concerned over the increasing instances of rude behaviour towards staff, especially meal and playtime supervisors. They decided to take the following steps.

Step 1: In assembly and during class the children were told about respect. They were given examples through stories and shown examples of respectful behaviour.

Step 2: A team of Year 6 children were given a project to record or photograph examples of respectful behaviour around the school. Examples included, doors been held open for other people, children and adults saying 'Please' and 'Thank you' when asking for assistance or receiving it. The results were made into large displays that were put up in classrooms and around the school.

Step 3: The children were told that for two weeks whenever staff – teaching and support staff – saw the children showing respect, those involved would be given a raffle ticket. All tickets were placed in a drum.

Step 4: After careful thought, the staff decided that drawing out an overall winner would not be appropriate. Instead each class had their own draw and then the winner from each class had the special privilege of handing out prizes to all the children for recognition for their efforts in taking part in Project Respect. Everyone was therefore a winner.

The staff and children considered this to have been a useful and important project and the number of rude behaviours, especially during playtimes, were reduced dramatically.

This approach highlights the benefit of explaining to children what respect is and why it is important, showing them examples of respect and then enabling them to practise being respectful while earning recognition at the same time.

Response Cost

This involves the offender, who has been disrespectful, being offered points for successful interactions either in the classroom or playtimes. An agreed number of points earns a reward. Punitive consequences, such as missing a playtime, are given for instances of disrespect.

Empathy Training

Teach the emotional consequences of the behaviour. Not an easy task, but one that will have a much more meaningful impact. Some empathy training methods are as follows:

Modelling   This technique involves the learner either watching videos or listening to stories and trying to predict the consequences of certain behaviours as well as the feelings that these would typically cause in people.

Self-awareness Training   This involves the learner being given a list of feelings words and then matching the words to different situations. For example, 'anger'

Social

or 'sadness' at their bike being stolen, 'happiness' and 'pleasure' at winning a holiday in a competition, and 'kindness' and 'caring' at helping a friend out of a difficulty.

Fantasy Techniques   A story is made up where the central character behaves in positive and negative ways. These are made similar to the behaviours that the focus child has been displaying. The learner is given the role of director with agreed consequences for both disrespectful and respectful behaviours, thereby allowing the child to learn through controlling the positive or negative outcomes for the character.

Respect Through Restorative Justice   Restorative justice is a method of 'making up for messing up'. If we consider that school staff are not meant to be custodians of learners but educators for them, then this approach is ideal. When learners make behavioural mistakes such as being rude and disrespectful to either adults or peers, then they should not only say 'sorry', but be helped to make up for the hurt and upset that has been caused. The adult asks such questions as, 'What did you do?', 'What were the consequences?', 'What can be done to make up for this?' and finally, 'What can be learnt to do next time?' This approach turns a behavioural mistake into a learning opportunity, learners can see that there are consequences to their behaviours and they have to take responsibility for the behavioural choices they make.

Discussion Questions

More mature learners could be encouraged to discuss such questions as:

- How do you think you would feel if someone judges you without knowing you or giving you a chance? How do you feel when someone you disagree with calls you a rude name? How do you feel when someone bumps into you in the playground and doesn't say 'sorry'?

- Discuss this statement and agree or disagree giving reasons: 'Courtesy and politeness are a load of nonsense'.

- 'If someone shows you respect, you should show respect in return'. Do you agree? How do you feel if you treat someone with respect and that person responds with rudeness? If someone insults you, should you insult that person in return?

- What are the benefits of treating each other with respect?

- Watch a television programme, and then discuss whether you think the characters were respectful or disrespectful.

- Describe three things you could do to be a more respectful person. How would that affect your relationships with others? What are the gains to you for being a respectful person?

Social

- Think of as many ways as you can to make your school environment more respectful.

- Make a list of the benefits of being respectful and another for the disadvantages of being disrespectful. Describe what a class would look like if it followed one or the other. How would people behave towards each other and what would the consequences be?

These questions can also be printed off from the CD Rom and used as a group exercise.

Skill Deficits

Alternatively, if the lack of respect is considered to be a skill deficit, this means that the learner has not learnt such skills as sharing, taking turns, or saying 'Please' and 'Thank you'. There is no need to know the reasons for this deficit and the failure to acquire these skills because the aim is to help the child learn them.

You may find it helpful to start by answering the following Skill Assessment Profile, which is available to print from the CD-Rom.

 Does the child/young person:

1 Lack the necessary social skills in many situations? YES/NO

2 Seem motivated to improve his/her relationships? YES/NO

3 Frequently become involved in disputes with peers? YES/NO

4 Relate better to children younger than him/herself? YES/NO

5 Not improve the behaviour when sanctioned? YES/NO

6 Appear keen to make friends and please adults? YES/NO

7 Enjoy being with adults? YES/NO

8 Avoid playtimes when possible? YES/NO

9 Prefer individual learning tasks? YES/NO

10 Have a history of relationship problems? YES/NO

If the scoring results in five or more YES answers then there is a clearer indication that the problem is a skill deficit.

There are many excellent resources for developing social skills in children and young people (Casey, 2002) The specific skills that may be required in either the classroom or the playground are obviously extensive, so the general method discussed here will be influenced by the work of Furman (2004) and Strayhorn (1988). Often it can be the problem or deficit that is studied and analysed, whereas it is the solution to the problem that needs to be better understood:

> we do not devote much time to finding out the original cause of the child's difficulty. Instead we focus on what the child needs to learn, thus avoiding those typical fault finding conversations so characteristic of more traditional approaches to childhood issues. (Furman, 2004: 8)

For example, if a learner is fighting, the aim is not to analyse and stop the fighting, but to teach the necessary skills of sharing, cooperation and the settling of differences in a constructive way. It is not necessary to know the cause/s of a problem to solve it. The key question should always be 'What are the skill/s this learner needs in order to not have the problem?' A much more positive and constructive approach.

Developing Social Skills

Step 1: Setting Goals   This first step needs to be carefully worked through. Too large a goal will result in failure and demotivation of all involved. The aim is to turn the problem into an achievable solution and to find those skills that the learner needs to not have the problem. For example, the school wants children to walk between classes instead of running, the preferable notices for the school to display should read WALK. That is the behaviour that the school wishes to encourage. The key question is 'What does the child need to learn for the problem to disappear?' (Furman, 2004)

 Case Study 5.10   Jody, 8 years old

> In class, Jody frequently shouts out across the class to other children. The problem is clear, but Jody needs to learn to wait until breaktime to share information with her friends for the problem to be solved. The goal will be 'sharing news at breaktime'.

If the problem is large then the approach is to break it up into several sub-skills to be learnt. For example, the problem behaviour of poor concentration could be tackled through various tasks – staying in one place for a set time, listening without interrupting, waiting one's turn to speak and putting a hand up to make a class contribution. Success is more achievable by breaking down the behaviour and working on one small goal at a time.

Step 2: Model It   Human beings of all ages copy behaviour patterns that they see (Strayhorn, 1988). Depending on the skill to be learned, provide the pupil with as many examples as possible. Sitting the child by another learner who already has the skill can help the focus child to see and copy what is to be achieved.

Step 3: Give Directions   School staff should sit with the learner and carefully explain and describe the skills that are to be learned. For example, the practitioner might say to the learner, 'When you are in the playground and want to join in a game, it is good to watch how the game is being played and then approach one of the players and ask if it is all right to join in'. Being clear and direct about the skill to be developed is a positive way to help a learner understand exactly what skill is required.

Step 4: Practise   Any skill that has been mastered has always been achieved following a certain amount of practice. Once a learner has a clear idea of the skill to be developed and can demonstrate it, there should then be a period when opportunities are provided for the skill to be practised in a range of situations. At first, ensure that the situation is familiar to the learner and one where there is a certain guarantee of success – nothing breeds success, like success. Gradually increase the demands of the situation – maybe including children that the learner knows less well.

Step 5: Monitor   Following practice, the second most important feature of learning a new skill is feedback – this informs the individual how well he/she is doing. The practitioner needs to have frequent talks with the learner to review progress, how well the situation is going and which areas might need more practice.

Step 6: Recognition/rewards   In discussion with the learner, agree some positive consequences for positive changes. Such rewards can be seen as feedback to the learner, telling him/her that the right track is being taken and that good progress is being made.

Step 7: Attribution   The final step is when the progress made is translated into terms of the learner's personal traits and qualities. The aim is to help the learner appreciate that the skill has been mastered through personal effort and determination. Unfortunately, this type of achievement can often be explained away by many children and adults as being due to luck, or because other people were helping. It is important to help the learner understand that he/she is responsible for mastering this skill. It is then more likely for the learner to face the next goal with a genuine belief in his/her abilities to succeed.

These ideas will enable the practitioner to tackle the two different categories of problems in social skills – performance-related and skill deficit. With these two models, the practitioner can approach any social skill issue as a learning opportunity, but if any interventions are to be successful, there are certain conditions that will increase the likelihood of success in both areas. Firstly, does the learner have some insight into the need for different social behaviours in different social contexts? Secondly, are there numerous opportunities for the learner to practise the skills, and, thirdly, can the new skills be consistently and sensitively rewarded and encouraged?

Conclusion

It is evident that much learning in schools takes place through cooperative learning. It is vital therefore that all learners are able to relate in a positive manner with their peers. Those who lack these skills face serious difficulties. It should be noted that there will be a minority of learners who have both performance and skill deficits linked together, and it will take time and determination for such problems to be mastered.

Social

Happiness

Happiness Tools

As has already been discussed, happiness is a difficult concept to define, but this does not mean that it is impossible to be used as a valuable set of tools, completing the multifaceted approach to in-school problem behaviour. Philosophers can continue to theorise about the concept of happiness, but it is techniques to improve happiness that are required in the final section of this multifaceted intervention Toolbox.

When to use Happiness Tools?

The importance of happiness is relevant for all learners who have scored four or above in the assessment questionnaire. This means that this set of tools will probably be the most used. Helping learners to understand that happiness is not something that just happens but is a set of skills that can be learned and practised, must be a worthwhile goal for any practitioner.

The Tools

Positive Memories
With the practitioner, the young person produces a booklet with details of two or more happy memories, including as much detail as possible. Where were they? Who were they with? What were they doing and what were they wearing? Research shows that people who are depressed have difficulty recalling pleasant memories and instead go over and over negative memories – thereby increasing their unhappiness. Use the booklet frequently to encourage the child to establish positive memories.

At Your Best

The practitioner works with the young person to find a time when he/she was at their best – maybe playing a ball game or drawing. Ask the child to:

- Think of a time when you were at your best, or a time when you were making something.

- What were you doing and what skills were you using?

The practitioner may have to help the child understand the skills that were being used, such as playing as a team member or planning how to make something. Help the child to either write or draw it in detail.

For the next week, the practitioner reviews the 'at your best' time once every day and reflects with the learner the strength/s identified.

Acts of Kindness
The act of helping is of 'paramount importance for mental health' (Strayhorn, 1988). Strayhorn refers to the process of a child helping others, or being helped or observing acts of kindness. Altruistic acts and happiness seem to go together. It is recognised that some altruistic acts can be undertaken for personal gain – false altruism – but true disinterested altruism, where it is the outcome that matters and

not personal satisfaction, has a genuine positive effect. Altruism can be defined as one person's efforts to increase the welfare of another, and it is often motivated by the human ability to empathise with another person's distress. Most children naturally develop this ability through having secure attachments to their carers and being raised in a warm and supportive home environment. Empathy can also be encouraged by helping children to reflect on the impact of their behaviour on others. The learner could:

- help another learn a skill

- take care of a school pet

- help staff with specific tasks.

Badge of Courage

This technique involves the young person learning about personal strengths and qualities. It reminds the child of challenges that have been faced and the progress that has been made. It involves the young person – with support – answering the following questions:

- What was a challenge/fear faced?

- How long did I face this challenge?

- How many times have I faced this challenge?

- What did I do to help me face it?

- What skills and personal qualities does it show I have?

It is important that a very concrete specific situation is explored. The aim of the badge is to provide the young person with very clear information about his/her own ability to cope and master personal challenges – for example, approaching a group and asking to join in a game, staying calm and focused before a test.

The badge is intended to help a young person break old behaviour patterns through stimulating positive memories of past successes. If viable, a photograph of the young person actually coping with the challenge could be included, this would enable them to literally picture themselves coping successfully.

Signature Strengths

While a young person will, like each of us, have weaknesses and difficulties, it is more important and uplifting for the focus to be on their abilities and strengths.

> I do not believe that you should devote overly much effort to correcting your weaknesses. Rather, I believe that the highest success in living and the deepest emotional satisfaction comes from building and using your signature strengths. (Seligman, 2003: 13)

The practitioner helps the young person select his/her top five strengths. The list below is an aide-memoire and can be added to.

- Listening to others

- Sharing

- Cooperating

- Helping others

- Singing

- Sport.

For each of the top five strengths, ask the child to consider:

- Do I feel good/excited when I display it?

- Do I look for ways to display this skill?

- Do I lose any sense of time when doing it?

Make sure the young person has time to display this skill.

Solution-Focused Thinking

This technique is competency based as it helps young people to notice and name their own personal resources and strengths. In fact, it is these attributes that enable them to make progress. At the heart of solution-focused thinking are three principles:

1   Do more of what is working and less of what is not.

2   The 'ripple effect' – a small change can have a big impact.

3   It is future focused – creating pictures of how an individual wants things to be in the future.

How is This Achieved?   Enable the young person to find exceptions to his/her general day-to-day feelings – those times when he/she felt good, alive, excited about him/herself. Ask the child to rate himself on a scale from 1 to 10 as to how he feels at the moment (1 feeling low and 10 feeling very good). Where are you just now? What are you doing right to put yourself where you now are? What can you start doing to improve matters? What does the young person need to do more of to improve things?

Solution-focused thinking encourages the young person to see his/her own coping skills and resilience. The process generates positive emotions that will counteract the negative ones associated with sadness, depression and a lack of success.

Tasks   Observational tasks – ask the young person to recognise times when he/she felt happier than usual.

Pretend tasks – ask the young person to pretend that he/she is happier. Discuss what it feels like, what would he/she do, how would he/she smile, etc. Then, set a task of practising 'pretending'.

Happiness

Setting Goals   It is helpful as early as possible to set goals for the young person to be working on. A simple, but useful model comes from coaching (Allen, 2006). The GROW model works as follows.

Goal – what is the goal the young person would like to work towards?

Reality – where is the young person on the path towards that goal now?

Options – what could the young person do to move towards the goal?

Will – what actions will the young person set in place?

Anchoring Technique

The practitioner explores with the learner a happy memory from his/her past. Ask him/her to describe the situation in as much detail as possible. Where is he/she? Who is he/she with? What is he/she wearing? What can he/she see? What can he/she smell? Is he/she inside or outside? Now ask the learner to look inside himself and describe his feelings. The final step is to associate this pleasurable and happy feeling inside with something that can remind him of the feeling in difficult times. It could be a word, a pebble, or just crossing his fingers – this is the 'anchor.' The learner then practises throughout the day using the anchor to remind him of how to feel happy.

Positive Event Planner

Unhappy children are prone to anhedonia, that is, a decreased interest in pleasurable activities which is perfectly natural in the circumstances. The following technique involves finding out from the young person the activities that he/she used to enjoy. This will not be an easy task, but if the child is not able to make suggestions try exploring what peers do for fun, for example, playing football, riding a bike, skateboarding.

The aim now is to schedule some more of these events into the young person's week. Make it clear how long the child is expected to engage in the activity. Create a weekly chart, with pictures or drawings of the activity, pinned to the day when it is to take place. For example, Saturday could have a picture of ice-skating.

Increasing Pleasure and Competency

Children and young people with low self-esteem tend to reduce their involvement in pleasure and mastery type activities. That is, those activities in which pleasure is obtained because they are fun to do, and/or competency or mastery comes from skills that enable children to do set tasks.

The aim is to increase the child's involvement in these type of activities. Ask the child/young person to complete a record of activities for each hour over a week. Use the template included on the CD-Rom. Then, rate each key activity undertaken in any hour, as to whether it involved P (pleasure) or C (Competency). Ask the child to rate how much pleasure or competency each activity has on a scale of 1 to 10, with 1 indicating little; 5 reasonable; 10 a lot. Help the child to do more of those activities with higher scores.

Evocative Music

With the learner, the practitioner explores different music that evokes strong feelings of pleasure for the young person. Set him/her the task of practising hearing the chosen music in his/her head at specific times of the day.

Pleasure Predicting

The practitioner plans with the young person an activity that he/she expects to enjoy. Ask the child to rate from 1 to 10 how much fun he/she expects to have doing the activity (1 being little fun, 10 being lots of fun). After the activity ask the child to think about how much fun he/she actually felt.

It is common for young people who are depressed to predict a low level of enjoyment prior to an event and then to be pleasantly surprised at the actual level of enjoyment that was experienced.

Conclusion

Including the happiness tool means that this Toolbox has gone further than just considering the technical skills that education offers and that learners require.

> A good education is one that fosters, among other things, social and emotional competence, communication skills, wisdom, resilience and a lifelong love of learning. There is far more to education than just acquiring qualifications. (Martin, 2006: 231)

Useful Websites

Physiological

Youth Information – the information toolkit for young people
www.youthinformation.com

Every Child Matters – change for children
www.everychildmatters.gov.uk

Feelings

Antidote – making change possible
www.antidote.org.uk

teachernet – The Social and Emotional Aspects of Learning (SEAL)
www.teachernet.gov.uk/seal

Young Minds
www.youngminds.org.uk

Behaviour

Behaviour Matters
www.teachingexpertise.com

Social, Emotional and Behavioural Difficulties Association
www.sebda.org

Thinking

counselling children and young people
www.ccyp.co.uk

Mental Health – information and links
www.mindinfo.co.uk

Social

kidscape – helping to prevent bullying and child abuse
www.kidscape.org.uk

Inclusive Solutions
www.inclusive-solutions.com

Happiness

authentic happiness
www.authentichappiness.sas.upenn.edu

child of our time
www.open2.net/childofourtime/2007/index.html

References

Adler, A. (1969) *The Practice and Theory of Individual Psychology*. Paterson, NJ: Littlefield.

Adler A. (1992) *Understanding Human Nature*. Oxford: Oneworld.

Allen L. (2006) *Behind with the Marking and Plagued by Nits*. Carmarthen, Wales: Crown House.

Aronson, E. (1997) *The Social Animal*. London: WH Freeman and Co.

Asch, S. (1955) 'Opinions and Social Pressure', *Scientific America*, 193: 2135.

Barkley, R. (1997) *ADHD and the Nature of Self-control*. New York: Guilford Press.

Bloomquist, M.L. and Schnell, S.V. (2005) *Helping Children with Aggression and Conduct Problems*. New York: Guilford Press.

Brallier, J. and Chabert, S. (1996) *Presidential Wit and Wisdom*. Harmondsworth: Penguin.

Bruner, J. (1973) *Beyond the Information Given*. New York: W.W. Norton.

Butler, G. and Hope, T. (1995) *Manage Your Mind*. Oxford: Oxford University Press.

Carr, A. (2004a) *The Handbook of Child and Adolescent Clinical Psychology*. Hove: Brunner-Routledge.

Carr, A. (2004b) *Positive Psychology*. Hove: Brunner-Routledge.

Carroll, L. (2005 [1872]) *Alice's Adventures in Wonderland and Through the Looking Glass*. Digireads.com

Casey, J. (2002) *Getting it Right: A Behaviour Curriculum*. Bristol: Lucky Duck.

Clough, P., Garner P., Pardeck, J.T. and Yuen, F. (eds) (2005) *Handbook of Emotional and Behavioural Difficulties*. London: SAGE.

Cooper, P.W. (2005) 'Biology and behaviour: the educational relevance of a biopsychosocial perspective', in P. Clough, P. Garner, J.T. Pardeck, and F. Yuen (eds) *Handbook of Emotional and Behavioural Difficulties*. London: SAGE. pp. 105–21.

Croll, P. and Hastings, N. (1996) *Effective Primary Teaching*. London: David Fulton.

Crone, D. and Horner, R. (2003) *Building Positive Behaviour Support Systems in Schools*. New York: Guilford Press.

Csikszentmihalyi, M. (1997) *Finding Flow*. New York: Basic Books.

Dawson, P. and Guare, R. (2004) *Executive Skills in Children and Adolescents*. London: Guilford Press.

Department for Education and Skills (2005) *Excellence and Enjoyment: Social and Emotional Aspects of Learning New Beginnings*. Norwich: HMSO.

Dodge, K., Bates, J. and Pettit, S. (1990) 'Mechanisms in the cycle of violence,' *Science*, 250: 1678–83.

Goleman, Daniel (1995) *Emotional Intelligence*. New York: Bantam Books.

Friedberg, G.R. and McClure, K. (2002) *Cognitive Therapy with Children and Adolescents*. New York: Guilford Press.

Freud, S. (1930) 'Civilisation and its discontents', in *The Standard Edition of the Complete Psychological Works of Sigmund Freud* (ed. and trans. by J. Strachey). London and New York: W.W. Norton.

Furman, B. (2004) *Kids' Skills*. Victoria, Australia: St Luke's Innovative Resources.

Gilbert, D. (2006) *Stumbling on Happiness*. London: Harper Press.

Hadley, M. and Rice, J. (1991) 'Predictions of interactional failure in preschool children', *Journal of Speech, Language and Hearing Research*, 34: 130817.

Haggerty, R., Sherrod, L., Garmezy, N. and Rutter, M. (1996) *Stress, Risk and Resilience in Children and Adolescents*. New York: Cambridge University Press.

Hanko, G. (1994) 'Discouraged children: when praise does not help', *British Journal of Special Education*, 21 (4): 166–8.

Hartas, D. (2005) *Language and Communication Difficulties*. London: Continuum.

Hetherington, E.M. (ed.) (1983) *Handbook of Child Psychology. Vol. 4: Socialization, Personality, and Social Development*. New York: Wiley. pp. 1–101.

Hock, R. (2005) *Forty Studies that Changed Psychology*. Englewood Cliffs, NJ: Prentice Hall.

Holowenko, H. (1999) *Attention Deficit/Hyperactivity Disorder*. London: Jessica Kingsley.

Kaiser, B. and Rasminsky, J. (2003) *Challenging Behaviour in Young Children*. Boston: Allyn and Bacon.

Ladd, G. and Mize, J. (1983) 'A cognitive-social learning model of social-skill training,' *Psychological Review*, 90: 127–57.

Martin, P. (2006) *Making Happy People*. Suffolk: Harper Perennial.

Marzano, R. (2003a) *Classroom Management that Works*. Alexandria, VA: Association for Supervision and Curriculum Development.

Milgram, S. (1964) *Obedience to Authority*. New York: Harper and Row.

Moser, A. (1988) *Don't Pop Your Cork on Mondays!* Kansas City: Landmark Editions.

Nicolson, D. and Ayers, H. (2004) *Adolescent Problems*. London: David Fulton.

Palmer, S. (2006) *Toxic Childhood*. London: Orion.

Pavlov, I. (1927) *Conditioned Reflexes*. Oxford: Oxford University Press.

Piaget, J. (1960) *The Child's Conception of the World*. London: Routledge.

Piper, W. (2005) *The Little Engine that Could*. New York: Philomel.

Roberts, R. (2002) *Self-Esteem and Early Learning. London*: Paul Chapman.

Rutter, M. and Smith, D. (eds) (1995) *Psychosocial Disorders in Young People*. Chichester: John Wiley and Sons.

Schwartz, M. and Andrasik, F. (2003) *Biofeedback*. London: Guilford Press.

SEAL Primary National Strategy (2005) *Excellence and Enjoyment: Social and Emotional Aspects of Learning*. Nottingham: DfES. Ref: DfES0110-2005G.

Seligman, M. (1996) *The Optimistic Child*. New York: Harper Perennial.

Seligman, M. (2003) *Authentic Happiness*. London: Nicholas Brealey.

Selye, H. (ed.) (1983) *Selye's Guide to Stress Research*. New York: Scientific and Academic Editions.

Sherif, M. (1936) *The Psychology of Group Norms*. New York: Harper.

Skinner, B. (1971) *Beyond Freedom and Dignity*. New York: Alfred Knopf.

Sperry, R.W. (1951) 'Mechanisms of neural maturation', in S.S. Stevens (ed.) *Handbook of Experimental Psychology*. New York: John Wiley and Sons. pp. 236–80.

Stallard, P. (2002) *Think Good Feel Good*. Chichester: John Wiley and Sons.

Strayhorn, J. (1988) *The Competent Child*. London: Guilford Press.

Stringer, B. and Mall, M. (1999) *Anger Management with Children*. Birmingham: Questions Publishing.

Vygotsky, L. (1962) *Thought and Language*. Cambridge, MA: MIT Press.

Watson, J.B. (1930) *Behaviourism*. Chicago, IL: University of Chicago Press.

Bibliography

Berg, I.K. and Steiner, T. (2003) *Children's Solution Work*. London: W.W. Norton and Company.

Betts, S., Betts, D. and Gerber-Eckard, L. (2007) *Asperger's Syndrome in the Inclusive Classroom: Advice and Strategies for Teachers*. London: Jessica Kingsley.

Blackburn, I. and Davidson, K. (1995) *Cognitive Therapy for Depression and Anxiety*. Oxford: Blackwell.

Edelstein, B. and Michelson, L. (1986) *Handbook of Prevention*. New York: Plenum Press.

Faupel, A., Herrick, E. and Sharp, P. (1998) *Anger Management*. London: David Fulton.

Fennell, M. (1999) *Overcoming Low Self-esteem*. London: Robinson.

Galvin, P. (1999) *Behaviour and Discipline in Schools: Practical, Positive and Creative Strategies for the Classroom*. London: David Fulton.

Galvin, P., Miller, A. and Nash, J. (1999) *Behaviour and Discipline in Schools: Devising and Revising a Whole School Policy*. London: David Fulton.

Herbert, M. (1992) *Clinical Child Psychology*. Chichester: John Wiley and Sons.

Hopkins, B. (2004) *Just Schools*. London: Jessica Kingsley.

Huppert, F., Bayliss, N. and Keverne, B. (2005) *The Science of Well-being*. Oxford: Oxford University Press.

Layard, R. (2005) *Happiness*. Harmondsworth: Penguin.

Lopez, S.J. and Snyder, C.R. (2004) *Positive Psychological Assessment*. Washington, DC: American Psychological Association.

McNamara, S. (2000) *Stress in Young People*. London: Continuum.

Marzano R. (2003b) *What Works in Schools*. Alexandria, VA: Association for Supervision and Curriculum Development.

Moghaddam, F. (2005) *Great Ideas in Psychology*. Oxford: Oneworld.

O'Regan, F. (2007) *Teach and Manage Children with ADHD*. Cambridge: LDA.

Porter, L. (2007) *Behaviour in Schools: Theory and Practice for Teachers*. Maidenhead: Open University Press.

Rutherford, R., Quinn, M. and Mathur, S. (2004) *Handbook of Research in Emotional and Behavioural Disorders*. London: Guilford Press.

Scotto, J. and Meyer, H. (1999) *Behavioural Intervention*. Baltimore, Maryland: Brookes Publishing.

Sommers-Flanagan, J. and Sommers-Flanagan, R. (1997) *Tough Kids, Cool Counselling*. Alexandria, VA: American Counselling Association.

Vizard, D. and Vizard, T. (2007) *A Guide to Syndromes and Conditions*. Abbotskerswell, Devon: Behaviour Solutions.

Wearmouth, J., Richmond, R.C. and Glynn, T. (2004) *Addressing Pupils' Behaviour*. London: David Fulton.

Wearmouth, J., Richmond, R.C., Glynn, T. and Berryman, M. (2004) *Understanding Pupil Behaviour in Schools*. London: David Fulton.

Whitehouse, E. and Pudney, W. (2006) *A Volcano in My Tummy*. Canada: New Society.

Index